THE MAN FROM KRYPTON

THE MAN FROM KRYPTON

THE GOSPEL ACCORDING TO SUPERMAN

JOHN WESLEY WHITE

Foreword by
BILLY GRAHAM

Bethany Fellowship INC.
MINNEAPOLIS, MINNESOTA 55438

The Man from Krypton
John Wesley White

Library of Congress Catalog Card Number 78-73455

ISBN 0-87123-384-3

Copyright © 1978
John Wesley White
All Rights Reserved

Published by Bethany Fellowship, Inc.
6820 Auto Club Road, Minneapolis, Minnesota 55438

Printed in the United States of America

Preface

When in the autumn of 1978, for the second time in thirty-four days, the one hundred and eleven cardinals of the Roman Catholic Church locked themselves away in conclave to choose as pope, John Paul II, a commentator of world stature urged them to try to select a "superman," someone who could survive the terrifying pressures which had apparently prematurely brought on the death of Pope John Paul I after little more than a month in office.

When a 455-year precedent of Italian pontiffs was broken and a Polish pope from the Communist world was chosen, it was quite electrifying to hear his reception announcement: "May Jesus Christ be praised." But it was his inauguration homily delivered via TV to the largest audience in the history of the world ever to hear a religious address which revealed unmistakably whom the new Pope deemed to be the Real Superman. In Italian he exclaimed, "Do not be afraid to welcome Christ and to accept His authority. Have no fear; open the doors—fling them open to Christ and to His saving authority. Open the confines of the states, of the economic and political systems, of the vast fields of culture. Civilization and development have no fear. Christ knows what is behind man. Only He knows." Then, in Polish, French, English, German, Spanish, Portuguese, Russian, Ukranian, Czech, and Lithuanian, he implored, "Men, open up your hearts to the Lord!"

Antichrist as projected in the prophetic scriptures will both compare and be in contrast to Jesus Christ. Superman can be both compared and contrasted to both! Whether in the tragic real life of a monstrous Jim Jones, or in the surrealistic fictionalizing of a Superman, Pascal's God-shaped blank in the human psyche is currently being exploited to the hilt. While the comparisons to the true Christ can be vividly depicted in these often defective characters, whether factual, in the case of a Jim Jones, or fictional, as in the case of Superman, one thing is evident: their degeneration is inevitable. Jim Jones went from Disciples of Christ clergyman to the devil's disciples, in which role he incited the suicide of nearly a thousand obsessed souls. Superman, starting as an exclusively savior figure a generation ago (as did Zeus of Greece and Jupiter of Rome) in Superman 1, is being gradually depraved until in Superman 2, 3, etc., he no doubt will follow the media and the masses into the moral morass of our times. It seems inevitable.

All of this is not the point of this book. What we're here examining is how desirous current man is for a Christ, any Christ. Our intent is to point people to the true Christ: Jesus our Lord.

November, 1978   John Wesley White

Contents

Chapter 1	Superman	11
Chapter 2	Supermaniac	22
Chapter 3	Superbaby	46
Chapter 4	Super Doer	57
Chapter 5	Super Lover	71
Chapter 6	Super Seer	93
Chapter 7	Super Sonic	112
Chapter 8	Super Supplier	131
Chapter 9	Superior Judge	149
Chapter 10	Super Savior	166

1
Superman

"Faster than a speeding bullet," trumpets the announcer as the gunshot ricochets. "More powerful than a locomotive!" booms the voice, as the sound of a thundering train is heard. "Able to leap tall buildings in a single bound. Look up at the sky; it's a bird!" shouts a man. "It's a plane!" exclaims a woman. "It's Superman!" explodes the voice over, and adds, "This Man of Steel. Defender of Justice. Righter of Wrongs. It's Superman!" A series of nostalgic awakening exclamations in the memories of most middle-aged North Americans. Right? Wrong! Not just memories!
Superman is back!!!

Forty years ago writer Jerry Siegel and artist Joe Schuster, who had been dreaming and scheming Superman since their teens, finally premiered their fictional brainchild in *Action Comics* and realized a total profit of $200 for their efforts. As the Great Depression gave way to World War II, Superman got his own comic book and turned up as a daily newspaper strip. In 1940 he made his debut on radio. Then he broke into pictures, and Paramount Studios and Max Fleischer produced seventeen short, full-color "Superman" cartoons between 1941 and 1943. George Lowther's novel, *Superman*, was published by Random House in

1942. And that was it for the duration of World War II.

Thirty years ago Kirk Alyn portrayed the Man of Steel in the serial, *Superman* (1948). It became the top money-making serial of all time!

In 1950 Superman began his seven-year saga on television, starring George Reeves. The Iowa-born actor had gone from *Gone with the Wind*, *World War II*, and *Samson and Delilah* to the red, yellow and blue costume of Superman. But a week before his proposed marriage to Lennone Lemmon he went upstairs in his Hollywood home, stripped naked, put a Luger to his head and shot himself. After holding the world transfixed for twenty years, "Superman" was dead!

Now he is back! After two decades Christopher Reeve is replacing George Reeves in the starring role of a motion picture spectacular, *Superman*, into which Warner Brothers has poured a record 33 million dollars for promotion alone. *Time magazine* describes *Superman* as "the most supersecret, super-publicized movie ever shot." Producer Alexander Salkin, in addition to the usual hoopla, is setting up mock phone booths in bookstores throughout the world (the kind that protect Superman's real identity when he doffs his Clark Kent duds). There will, of course, be records, gimmicks, toys, tee-shirts as well. And to top all that, there's a 90-minute TV special, complete with Brando and Hackman, with the primary aim of turning the masses from their television sets to the local movie houses to see the biggest mogul monster of all time. From what *The New York Times* labeled as a "passion for privacy," an incredible "aura of high secrecy" to keep *Superman* under wraps during its making stages, suddenly we're besieged with *Superman* publicity nearly as ubiquitous as the media itself.

So what do those who see the film encounter? For starters, there are four times the special effects of *Star*

Wars. There's Marlon Brando (he was paid $2 1/4 million to go to England for 12 days shooting in 1977). He's Jor-El, the father, who sends Superbaby down to earth from planet Krypton. There's superstar Gene Hackman who commands a similar salary for simulating the satanic Lex Luthor, whose archvillainness is Valerie Perrine, playing the tarty, tacky Eve. Then there's Margot Kidder as slim, hazel-eyed Lois Lane, Superman's sweetheart.

Superman himself is played by a relatively newcomer, Christopher Reeve. Reeve, 6'4", who spent some months in intensive body-building under the supervision of a former Mr. Universe to get his torso into Mr. Atlas shape, is the son of a Princeton professor. He is also a former hockey star, and bit player on TV's *Love of Life*. He was selected from among two hundred candidates, including Bruce Jenner, who auditioned for the part. Undoubtedly Reeve's primary qualification is his own personal commitment to the movie's assumed message. In an interview he seems almost to be standing outside himself when he says, "I prevent an earthquake. I repair Golden Gate bridge and Boulder Dam. I walk through fire and I prevent a nuclear explosion in Southern California." He insists that the sensational special effects are incidental. "Who cares about some guy in blue tights flying around? This story is about someone coming from far away, alone, with a purpose. What makes him a hero is how he uses his powers. It's about believing!"

Mario Puzo, author of *The Godfather*, wrote both the story and the screenplay for *Superman*, with assists from David and Leslie Newman and Robert Benton. The script was finally doctored into shape by Tom Mankiewicz. He says his vision for the film is that "whatever Jimmy Carter is asking us to be, Superman already is. What we are giving people is the

Christian message: that we should be honest, love one another, and be for the underdog." Director Richard Donner, who also directed *The Omen*, confesses candidly, "I was brought up on Superman and I believe this myth. There is a little of God bless America in it. There is purity and a fantasy in it that is right for our times." With this kind of conviction Donner cooly comments, "This is the biggest erector set, given to the biggest kid in the world."

As the movie unfolds we are initially introduced to a scene of Superman saving the life of Lois Lane. The news headline shouts, "Caped Wonder Stuns City!" Who is this muscular, huge-necked, broad-shouldered, jut-jawed man of steel in the shimmering blue body stocking emblazoned with the red and gold triangular "S," red trunks and boots? (He has at least 25 different costumes and 6 different kinds of capes to match the variety of situations and positions in which he is photographed.) It is Superman! After he drops her safely on her terrace, she prepares him an omelette and he cooks it with his X-ray eyes. Then he takes her on a 90-minute flight around the globe, and exhorts her to stop her chain smoking.

Of course this isn't where the real plot begins. Chronologically, the myth begins on planet Krypton in outer space, from which Superbaby is sent by his father.

When he arrives on earth he is adopted by Jonathan and Martha Kent. Three years later Jonathan is about to be crushed by a truck, and Superbaby intervenes, lifts up the back of the vehicle and saves his foster father's life. So Superbaby is emerging from the cocoon of childhood into Superman. Eventually, as Clark Kent, compelled by an irresistible urge, he goes to the North Pole and there builds his fortress of solitude where he communes with his father from Krypton. The scene between the two is, according to producer Salkind, a highly emotional one. "When Brando talks to his son the crowds weep." By repeated visits to his father in that remote place he is given full instructions. His father tells him who he is, and how his identity must never be divulged. He is told about his powers and how they are to be used only for good. He is commanded to "absorb all the world's wisdom" and then go to Metropolis and take a job as a newspaper reporter as ordinary, mild-mannered Clark Kent. After all, a newspaper is a good place to keep abreast of disasters!

The *Superman* producers first attempted to shoot in Rome, but the facilities proved too small so they went, instead, to the Shepperton Studios north of London for much of the footage. The fortress of solitude, for example, was the "007" stage of James Bond, with measurements of a mere mortal 374' by 160' by 53'. Eight of the Shepperton sound stages were utilized.

The *Daily Planet* newspaper offices were reconstructed in Iverheath in England, modelled after the depressingly realistic *New York Daily News*, with styrofoam cups half-filled with scum-covered coffee, trashy wastebaskets, heaped ashtrays, a non-functioning water cooler, long rows of littered desks, tattered dictionaries and all the debris of busy journalists left in disarray. Typewriters carry letterhead stationery reminding you that you're in the offices of *The Daily Planet*. It's a parable of how terrestrial, as well as celestial, the whole *Superman* film really is.

As Christopher Reeve insists, *Superman* is "about believing" and ties into the mood of our times. Pop singer Peter Frampton demonstrates this fact in his song of the year, "Show Me the Way." The lyrics articulate his generation's spiritual upreach: "Who do I believe in? I want you to show me the way. All I really want to know is that you will show me the way. Won't you please show me the way?" Billy Graham and Father Hesburgh, president of Notre Dame, were quoted jointly after a 1977 meeting: "The present generation of young people are more spiritually minded than any previous generation we've known."

In Canada the magazine *Quest* reckons that the church is doing much better "than they were a few years ago. The Anglicans, Roman Catholics, the United Church and the Presbyterians all enthuse over what they see as impressive new strengths in their own churches—fresh, strong interest in religion from young and old alike." These are the churches which had the biggest losses in the "iconoclastic sixties" when "attendance dropped off and so did the number of people who wanted to join the clergy." Of course it is well known that the smaller evangelical denominations in Canada are undergoing unprecedented growth in the seventies.

Goldfarb Consultants Ltd. have polled the Canadian people and discovered that 61% are convinced that "there is a turning toward religion today." It is interesting that 12% more of those who are under 35 years of age than of those over 35 believe that there's a turning to God. So the spiritual response today is largely among the young.

This is indeed quite significant as compared to the earlier half of the century when Carl Gustav Jung reckoned: "Among all my patients in the second half of life—that is to say over 35—there has not been one whose problem in the last resort was not that of finding a religious outlook on life." So that whereas the successor to Freud urged his patients toward the church in the latter half of their lives, today's spiritual response tends to be even stronger among the young than among older people.

Not only are the Divine and the Devil in *Star Wars*, but also DELIVERANCE. *Star Wars* has a Messiah figure called Kenobi, who is all wise, good and powerful. However, he does not triumph in his life. His victory comes when he is slain in a terrible battle with evil. Only his robe remains as he disappears. But his presence thereafter is what turns the tide. The energy for all feats of good is provided by The Force, which energy is wielded against the threat of annihilation from the Death Star. The people who are called to do battle against evil are led by Luke Skywalker, who is bored with farming on a remote planet, and Leia, who is a bride to be rescued. Both make total commitments to Kenobi and The Force.

In the end they win the battle for the Galaxy. The analogies here with the Christian faith are immediately evident.

So Kenobi is the messiah of *Star Wars*. But *Star Wars* is now superseded by *Superman*. And the writers came out deliberately and said they aspired to see *Superman* be a promotion of the Christian faith.

Certainly our generation has been inundated with Saviour figures in the entertainment world—especially on the screen. There's been Tarzan, Batman, Robin, Flash Gordon, Spiderman, Captain Marvel, the Green Hornet, the Thin Man, the Shadow, the Invisible Man, and the Six Million Dollar Man. What are they but Hollywood trying to simulate what man in his heart knows he needs: a saviour?

No doubt about it, *Superman*, the movie, arrives at a propitious time for such an idea. Bjorn Borg wins three Wimbletons to become a tennis giant. The press description? "Superman (Borg) is Everywhere." A baseball superstar is dubbed as the "Messiah." On the cover of *Time* magazine (June 19/78) Howard Jarvis, who crusaded through California for the Proposition 13 bill, is labelled "Maniac or Messiah?" Gore Vidal publishes his best-seller *Messiah,* which is touted as "the story of the coming of a new messiah promoted and publicized by radio and television."

Professor Milton Everett of Syracuse University, having invested a lifetime of scholarship in the study of religious cults, reckons that 30 million North Americans have gone into messiah corrals or messiah worshipping cults in the last few years. His colleague, Professor Buirati, calculates that there are currently over 2,000 masquerading messiahs in North America. Prime Minister Trudeau tells us candidly, "There's going to be not less authority in our lives" but more. He says that soon people, listening to and watching TV stations, will take their lead from whoever gets control of that electronic cannon—and a dictatorship may very well move in. The Bible says that dictator will be a world dictator. He will be the Antichrist, about whom *The Omen* or any number of films thematically are, have been, and will yet be made. Dr. Charles Beck, of the Faculty of Medicine, University of Calgary, has taken up the theme of how ripe Canadian society is today for a messiah figure who will then evolve into a Führer. He points to our craze for the Bionic Woman, Kojak, Police Woman, King Kong, astrology, and the macho-gun subculture. Dr. David Suzuki, our most lauded Canadian Geneticist/Physician/broadcaster suggests seriously we all keep scanning our horizon with ceaseless diligence for the ominous appearance of an "authoritarian personality." He's coming!

It is significant that Roman Catholic Archbishop Pakiam AroKiaswamy of India said during his recent visit to North America that he was shocked how Westerners were clutching desperately at "the trinkets of Eastern cults with their Christ figures, while bypassing the Pearl of Greatest Price, Jesus Christ. I can only believe that they've never been in Christ, or they would realize that their spiritual hungers can never be satisfied by anyone but Christ, who alone gives the gift of the Holy Spirit—true peace and joy."

I recently saw a book on a newstand entitled *The Search for Superman.* Everyone in his heart is searching—as a former U.N. President, Dr. Charles Malik, says—searching for Jesus Christ. A former Cabinet Minister reckons: "The world is scheming, groaning, travailing for someone who has a powerful voice of decisiveness; of authority that will give direction to a world that is stumbling around in the quagmire." David Hayes writes in *The Toronto Star:* "Canada is looking for a new leader . . . a miracle worker." Mr. Hayes, Jesus is that miracle worker. In *The Canadian Magazine,* Karsh of Ottawa, foremost photographer in the world, was asked whom he'd most like to photograph. "Jesus!" was his reply. Horowitz, the pianist, described as the world's greatest, was asked who he thought could play the piano better than he. "Jesus!" was his reply. Jesus can put harmony into an untuned life which is filled with discord. And as the title of Chuck Gerard's pop song goes: "He's Something Supernatural."

2

Supermaniac

In the *Superman* movie we are introduced to a creation which initially was unmistakably God's work: good, wholesome, positive! But evil, in the person of Lex Luthor (Gene Hackman), enters to corrupt and destroy. A real estate speculator, Director Donner describes how Luthor "lives under metropolis because he's too cheap to invest in above-ground property." Actually, there are "*three* super-villains, originally from Krypton," and they all possess supernatural powers. They are the counterparts of the three earth villains who team up to practically destroy the world. But global tragedy is averted in the knick of time, thanks to Superman. "Our Superman," emphasizes Donner, "saves the world." One would almost think he was reading from the book of Revelation. In chapters sixteen, nineteen and twenty we're told that that trinity of evil, the Devil, the beast, and the false prophet, almost gain possession of the world, but Christ comes in time to rescue the world and throw the diabolical troika into hell.

But, let's go back and pick up on the fact that the earth was initially created by God. It was good. It was intended as a place for man to live in harmony with God.

The Bible tells us that God made all things for himself. As Paul wrote to the Colossians: "For by him were all things created, that are in heaven, and that are in earth, visible and invisible, whether they be thrones, or dominions, or principalities, or powers: all things were created by him and for him: and he is before all things, and by him all things consist" (Col. 1:15-17).

God and His creation is a theme demanding renewed attention the world over in this the final quarter of the 20th century. "My life's ambition," said Moraji Desai when he became the Prime Minister of India, "is not to be Prime Minister, but to seek truth and realize God." This from a man in whose hands are the temporalities of 600 million people, spread over a nation of continental size. In a country like Poland, which is ruled by an allegedly atheistic communist regime, 99% of the population believe in a personal God and, as Billy Graham finds out in late 1978, their faith is vigorous. Even in Russia, despite a violently hostile regime, the Institute for Scientific Atheism recently publicly acknowledged for the first time that the number of underground Christian groups is growing rapidly, and that it is increasingly difficult to control rabid fanatics who believe that God is a person.

It is revealing that the traditionally liberal Michigan State University sets a spreading precedent for state universities by introducing a brand new course on "The Biblical Creation Story." The President enthusiastically insisted that it is true scholarship to put such a position before students as a basis for making up their own minds. A leading physicist with Columbia and Dartmouth Universities and the National Aeronautics and Space Administration in the United States, Dr. Jastrow reckons that despite the fact that most scientists hate the idea, yet theories about the nature of the universe point directly to a God so powerful He can produce the kind of energy needed to create a universe. Most scientists, he points out, attempt to maintain abstraction regarding the origin of the universe by trying to explain that the explosion of creation was only part of an endless cycle. Creation, insists Dr. Jastrow, occurred only once. The Bible begins: "In the beginning God created the heavens and the earth" (Gen. 1:1). So there is definitely a gathering momentum of support in the world scientific community for the creationist view.

The late Dr. Werner Von Braun became a Christian late in life. A friend of mine talked to him about his experience of Christ. He was already the number-one space scientist of all time and the acknowledged father of modern rocketry. But Dr. Von Braun was worried both about creation (its origin, meaning and destiny) and about his own relationship to his Creator. One day a cleaning woman left a Bible open to the book of Job. Dr. Von Braun casually—let's say providentially—picked it up. He read of the infinitude of the stars: "That's my position!" he thought. So he read on until he reached John's Gospel and there Dr. Von Braun paused and accepted Christ not only as his Creator but also as his Savior and his Lord.

A house is built for a family, a nation for a people. So God designed His universe for an order of living beings. Scientists today who subscribe to the "Big Bang" theory reckon that the original creation took place perhaps 16 billion years ago. Then at some point between then, which we might label as day one of the physical universe (the interstellar system), and the appearance of man on this planet (a period which biblically fits between Genesis 1:1 and Genesis 1:2) the original creation of living beings took their places in the physical universe.

Perhaps the most revered astronomer in the world is Sir Fred Hoyle, professor at the Royal Institute of Great Britain. In a 1978 article in the *New Scientist*, he insists that the usually accepted theory that the essential building blocks of life were formed in the "primeval soup" of primitive earth is now discredited. The origin of life, he avows, had to have happened somewhere in outer space—both of good and bad beings. He thinks—purely from a scientific point of view—that disease-spreading organisms are still coming in from outer space.

There are two main passages of scripture which indicate that there was a pre-Adamic creation of life inhabiting, not just the face of the earth, but the interstellar spaces. They are in Isaiah 14 and Ezekiel 28. In the latter we read, "In the day that thou wast created, thou art the anointed cherub that covereth; and I have set thee so; thou wast upon the holy mountain of God; thou hast walked up and down in the midst of the stones of fire [stars]. Thou wast perfect in thy ways from the day that thou was created, till iniquity was found in thee." Here obviously was Satan, or Lucifer, as he is referred to in Isaiah 14:12: "How art thou fallen from heaven, O Lucifer, son of the morning! How art thou cut down . . . for thou hast said in thine heart, I will ascend into heaven, I will exalt my throne above the stars of God: I will sit also upon the mount of the congregation, in the sides of the north; I will ascend above the heights of the clouds; I will be like the Most High. Yet thou shalt be brought down to hell, to the sides of the pit."

So, long, long ago—how long, we do not know—before Adam appeared on this planet—there was an innumerable array of angels headed by Satan. They were created, so they had a beginning. We read that they are indestructible, so that they are immortal. And Jesus said they do not marry—that is, they do not reproduce. It is my belief that every genuine UFO—most are hoaxes—every genuine UFO which is alive is an angel. In the Bible, angels appear in such a variety of forms and do such a variety of things that they account for the whole spectrum of bona-fide UFO and ESP activity in the universe today.

Jimmy Carter and Walter Cronkite are only two of the prominent North Americans who claim to have sighted UFOs. Since 1947 U.S. Air Force and University of Colorado scientists have investigated thousands of reported UFOs, stating candidly that 701 of them were inexplicable. According to a Gallup Poll in 1978, 57% of the Americans who've heard of UFOs believe they're real, while less than half that percentage—27%—think they're imaginary.

Articles on these and related themes are flooding the media, as we close out the seventies. *The New York Times* runs a long article on the speculation that 10 to 20 percent of the 100 billion or more stars forming the Milky Way galaxy probably have planets in orbit around them, any number of which could sustain life.

The idea that life, as we know it on earth, may exist elsewhere in the universe received a giant setback when it was seemingly demonstrated that Mars has had no such life as ours on earth. But that doesn't mean there aren't other kinds of life. *Time* (April 24/78) runs a feature on "Dabbling in Exotheology," in which a whole plethora of arguments are put forward that extraterrestrial life does exist elsewhere in the universe. A month later, letters to the Editor suggesting that two statements of Jesus would seem to imply this—i.e., that He identifies His own as existing "from one end of heaven to the other" (Matt. 24:31) and again, tells us "in my Father's house are many mansions" (John 14:2). To me the Scriptures clearly teach that God, in His original creation, created an order and hierarchy of angels, whose role was to operate the physical affairs of the interstellar spaces. Angels occupy a very significant place in the Scriptures, as Billy Graham points out in his best seller *Angels: God's Secret Agents*. It seems to me that the terrific curiosity and attention given in today's world—in both the East and West, Communist, and Capitalistic, academic and occult, scientific and superstitious, non-Christian as well as the Christian world—is a measure of what—and who—have to be out there. In mid-1978 the National Aeronautics and Space Administration (NASA) launched a five-year program to search the skies for possible radio signals from intelligent extraterrestrial civilizations. Known by the acronym SEI (Search for Extraterrestrial Intelligence), the program, using existing radio telescopes and the latest advances in computer technology, is an attempt to answer one of humankinds' oldest questions: "Are we alone in the universe?" The Russians, of course, launched such an inquiry earlier in the seventies: a nearly obsessive quest on their part. The Hearst newspapers in 1978 report that American astrophysicists who have been scanning the skies with radio telescopes since 1960, hunting for signs of extraterrestrial intelligence, say such radio leakage as ours can be detected and identified from as far away as 100 light years.

Indication of how widespread is the yearning of man to commune with extraterrestrial life could be seen in the spectacular success of the film *Close Encounters of the Third Kind*. It gave artificial respiration to all the fads and fancies about the paranormal:

the astrological, horoscopes, the mysteries of the Bermuda Triangle, Chariots of the Gods, thinking plants, and psycho-surgery. Not since 1938 when Orson Welles' *The War of the Worlds* hit the fan (in which millions of little green Martians were announced to have landed on earth) has there been such a commotion over invasions from outer space. Britons in 1978 are catapulted into hysteria as a normal BBC TV telecast in prime time is interrupted by a yet unexplained deep male voice, announcing himself as Asternon: "an authorized representative of the inter-galactic mission" warning mankind to "destroy its evil weapons" or they will destroy him.

To me, it is all quite clear. There is life throughout the universe: angelic life. Two-thirds of the angels are uncorrupted and acting as God's secret agents. The other third are a part of Satan's current army of demons; also called in Scripture, fallen angels.

Which returns us to Superman. Here is a monstrous corrupting character called Luthor, who degenerated God's good creation (as Darth Vader does in *Star Wars*) and is analogous to Satan.

Returning to Isaiah 14, we read: "How art thou fallen from heaven, O Lucifer, son of the morning! How art thou cut down." In Ezekiel, we read why: "Because thine heart is lifted up, and thou hast said, I am a God, I sit in the seat of God." So God said, "Because thou set thine heart as the heart of God," you shall be brought "down to the pit" (Ezek. 28: 2-8).

Jesus said to His disciples, "I beheld Satan as lightning fall from heaven" (Luke 10:18). So Lucifer was cast down, and a third of the angels with him. Why? "For thou hast said in thine heart, I will ascend into heaven, I will exalt my throne above the stars of God" (Isa. 14:13). In Ezekiel we read of Satan when he was "the anointed cherub that covereth [presided]" that "I [God] have set thee so: thou wast upon the holy mountain of God; thou hast walked up and down in the midst of the stones of fire [stars]. Thou wast perfect in thy ways from the day that thou wast created, till iniquity was found in thee . . . thou has sinned: therefore I will cast thee as profane out of the mountain of God: and I will destroy thee, O covering cherub, from the midst of the stones of fire. Thine heart was lifted up because of thy beauty, thou hast corrupted thy wisdom by reason of thy brightness: I will cast thee to the ground." (The base—i.e., the bottomless pit—something God will yet do.) "Thou hast defiled thy sanctuaries by the multitude of thine iniquities . . . therefore will I bring forth a fire from the midst of thee, and I will bring thee to ashes upon the earth in the sight of all them that behold thee. All they that know thee among the people shall be appalled at thee: thou shalt be a terror, and never shalt thou be any more" (Ezek. 28:14-19).

The Scriptures teach us that there are three heavens. The first heaven is the sky around the earth; the second, the interstellar space—all the physical universe; the third, the abode of God. Satan was charged with operational authority over the first and second heavens, but tried to ascend into the third—the Eternal God's eternal abode. This God could not and would not allow. But Satan never lost this craven ambition. When he tempted Jesus at the outset of our Lord's ministry here on earth, he was still asking Him to bow down and worship him, with the petty promise that if He would, he would give Him authority over the kingdoms of this world.

So Satan fell and all those vast hosts of evil emissaries with him. They are known variously in the Bible as devils, demons, evil spirits, unclean spirits and fallen angels. The late Pope Paul repeatedly pointed to the devil with his plethora of demons as the degenerating, disintegrating force undermining society throughout today's world. He called Satan "a living spiritual being, perverted and perverting. A terrible reality, mysterious and frightening."

His army is normally neither physically visible nor vocal. "The devil that you can't see is worse than the devil that you can see," lamented C. S. Lewis, considered by many to have been Britain's brightest brain. In his powerful *Screwtape Letters,* Lewis postulates a senior devil in hell communicating with a junior devil on earth named Wormwood, who in turn is tempting and taunting men throughout all nations and generations.

Of course, *Rosemary's Baby, The Exorcist* (which grossed $150 million), *The Exorcist II, The Omen, The Heretic* and any number of modern films have featured demonism in today's society. In 1978, *Time* (May 8, 1978) highlights the tragedy of a West German girl, Anneliese Michel, who died at the age of 23 in Kingenberg. When she passed away, she was little more than a skeleton, weighing a mere 68 pounds. Yet shortly before she died, her parents said Anneliese performed an astonishing 500 deep kneebends in one day. The source of her power, her parents believed, was nothing less than the devil himself. Anneliese's release from evil spirits came only with death, after she starved herself during a nightmarish ten-month series of exorcism rituals. The case came to court in Aschaffenburg. Two priests, Anneliese's parents, wealthy Mill Owner Josef Michel, 60, and his wife Anna, 57, were found guilty of negligent homicide. The four, who appealed their convictions, drew six-month suspended prison sentences. Here was a case in one of the most sophisticated societies, of demonism moving out of the classically fictional into the factual.

But demonism is to be seen not only in the overt but also in the covert. One of the most fascinating phenomena of the last ten years in the realm of religion has been the way Transcendental Meditation has come out of the East and crept up on the blind side of Western intellectuals. In the last chapter we looked at TM as a religion. I am convinced that it is satanic, demonic. A decade ago militant secularists—especially in our sophisticated universities—reached out to embrace TM as if they were greeting a long-lost cousin. There was the case of the very bright Toronto businessman who was until recently an instructor for the Maharishi Mahesh Yogi's transcendental meditation organization. He quit the movement when he was converted to Christ, realizing it had brought him into "slavery to occult, satanic forces." He has since been telling the story of his meeting with Jesus as Savior, whenever he can gain a hearing.

Withdrawal symptoms he claims, as he struggled to leave after seven years of meditating as much as 16 hours a day, were worse than those experienced by alcoholics or hard drug addicts. He asserts that his experiences in more than seven years of meditating have convinced him that the alleged claims of the TM'ers to supernatural powers "have some reality." He says he could read other people's minds, and even experience astral or soul travel when he was "high" on TM. He describes the sensation:

"You think you are controlling other, hidden forces in the universe, but frighteningly, I now believe they are actually controlling you."

Like many others in their teens and twenties during the late sixties, he was on a "spiritual search." A friend introduced him to TM, and, in the customary dimly lit room, with the picture of Guru Dev (the "divine teacher" of the maharishi) on a table, he knelt to receive his mantra. A mantra is a secret Sanskrit sound which the maharishi teaches his meditators to repeat softly during twice-daily 20-minute periods of meditation.

TM teachers say that each initiate receives his or her own unique mantra, but this man saw his teacher's list of 16 Hindu words or mantras given out on the basis of the initiate's age alone. They are not, as the maharishi insists, meaningless sounds, but the names of ancient Hindu deities or spirits. The maharishi insists further that they not be printed "lest people who don't know what they're doing try to experiment with them." After initiation, this man took a pilgrimage for a month to Maine. Here, in a rented summer resort on the coast, together with about 1,000 other young people, he was taught "rounding." This consists of a period of meditation, followed by yoga exercises and special breathing techniques. This threefold rite was performed some 10 to 12 times a day. "It produces a cumulative effect, growing to a peak. At the end you're so high you're bombed out of your mind."

A year later, again at his own expense, he spent three months with several thousand meditators on the island of Majorca. There they were taught to do "heavy rounding" for periods of up to 16 hours a day.

After several weeks of this, during which some kids "freaked out," the maharishi came and there were lectures, including instructions on how to initiate others. This man reckons his mind was "wiped so clear" by the heavy meditation that the idea of thinking for himself was "totally out of the question." He was given his list of 16 mantras and signed an official-looking document of loyalty to the maharishi and his now-dead Indian master, the "divine teacher."

Since the maharishi insists his movement is not religious, it is interesting to note the contents of the oath: "It is my fortune, Guru Dev, that I have been accepted to serve the Holy Tradition and spread the light of God to all those who need it. It is my joy to undertake the responsibility of representing the Holy Tradition in all its purity as it has been given to me by Maharishi and I promise on your altar, Guru Dev, that with my heart and mind I will always work within the framework of the organization founded by Maharishi. And to you, Maharishi, I promise that as a meditation guide I will be faithful in all ways to the trust you have placed in me."

This man in retrospect is still frequently alarmed at the strange psychedelic experiences he had. Once he recalls, "My body was lying there on the bed. I saw myself wake up, do a round of meditation, and then go out on the balcony before going back to bed. Somehow I was separated entirely from my mind as well as my body." On other occasions, he says, he was aware of shadowy forms and faces around him in the room at night. "Today I believe these were spirits of Hindu masters," he says. These, of course, were not his instructions. "You are told not to think about them, to remain passive. They call it 'unstressing' or cleansing of the nervous system."

He looks back on his mental state as he left Majorca, ready to initiate others, as that of a "philosophical zombie." He said: "My awareness was keen, but my conscience had been dulled completely. The overall mind-set was passive, unaware of any kind of evil." Having initiated some 500 converts into TM, our friend recalls that his real doubts about TM began, however, when he heard that the maharishi, who once taught his students to avoid psychic phenomena, had announced a "breakthrough of consciousness" in which people would be able to fly, become invisible, etc. Evidently the maharishi, whether by pre-design or for purposes of adaptation, "had changed direction 180 degrees. We were told explicitly by him to leave those things alone."

Noting that the maharishi has now set up a "World Plan" and a "World Government for the Age of Enlightenment," the former teacher says he is convinced the Indian yogi is on the "ultimate power trip," nothing less than control over the consciousness of humanity: a precursor to the Antichrist, no doubt.

Certainly the elaborate publication, *Creating an Ideal Society*, by the maharishi, speaks of his world government as being a "parent" to all other governments. He hallucinates: "The World Government for the Age of Enlightenment, with 1,500 capitals in 140 countries, consists of a legislative body, an executive body, a judicial body. . . . Since the sovereignty of the World Government lies in the domain of consciousness, the physical structure of the World Government is only meant to provide the basic channels through which pure consciousness, the field of supreme intelligence, can rule the world. . . ."

When this man, confronted by Christ, resolved to quit TM, he was subjected to a prolonged series of scary experiences in which the forms and spirits of previous encounters "assailed" him. "It was only when I asked Jesus Christ to come into my life and rid me of this nightmare that I found peace," he states. "I would like to see others experience the deliverance that has now been possible for me."

So whereas it would have seemed a discreditation to the academic community a generation ago to admit the presence all around us of a spirit world, it is generally accepted by intellectuals today. Comments Professor Arthur Gibson of the University of Toronto: "I'd be appalled if there weren't hundreds of kinds of intelligences in the universe, both in our atmosphere and on other planets." The popularity of such films as *The Outer Space Connection,* and *Starship Invasions* attest to this fact as do such best sellers as Erich Von Däniken's *Gods From Outer Space* and *Chariot of the Gods.* But does this all get to people? Take the Greater Toronto area, where Canada's leading talk showist, John Gilbert, holds forth to 250,000 people. Where does he get his advice? From the astrologer Katherine de Tersey! Stresses Gilbert: "I never do anything without consulting Katherine de Tersey."

How did the devil get started on man, on the planet earth? Returning to that Ezekiel 28:13 passage we read: "Thou hast been in Eden the garden of God." Here is a theme which has an incredible new popularity. Morris Dickstein entitles his best seller *Gates of Eden,* while C. Sagan's *The Dragons of Eden* tops the nonfiction best-seller list for much of 1978. At the same time the movies *Eden* and *Eve* can be seen advertised on nearly any big city theatre page.

So, we go back to the beginning chapters of the Bible to find out how Satan pulled the rug out from under the human race. There we read that God made man in His image and placed him in an ideal environment: the Garden of Eden, which means "pleasure, delight." The Garden of Eden was God's delight; it was for man's pleasure. There has never been a spot on earth, wrote the ancient prophet Joel (2:2), as "fair as Eden's Garden in all its beauty." The Biblical account in Genesis 2:7-22 tells us how God made the first man, Adam, and his wife, Eve. In their indescribably beautiful paradise, there were two conspicuous trees: the tree of life and the tree of the knowledge of good and evil. Enjoyment of the fruit of the former depended on abstinence from the fruit of the latter. Man, unlike the birds of the air, the animals of the field, or the fish of the sea, was made a free moral agent. He could choose to eat, or not to eat, of the fatal fruit. In their hands was the destiny of the entire human race.

So the ordeal of human history occurred. "The serpent [the devil] was the craftiest of all the creatures the Lord God had made." The serpent came to the woman. "Really?" he asked. "None of the fruit of the garden? You mean, God says you mustn't eat any of it?" Soon Eve, Adam, and then the whole human race, except for Christ himself, were into sin. The rock group "Blood, Sweat, and Tears" combined Mick Jagger's "Sympathy for the Devil" and Moussorgsky's "Night on Bald Mountain" in an album entitled "Sympathy for the Devil—Symphony to the Devil." Tragically and quickly Eve's sympathy for the devil had turned the human race into rendering a "symphony to the devil" which is playing and slaying at a higher decibel level today than the devil has directed in the long history of man.

Fred Kaeseker in reviewing *Full Circle*, featuring a demon-possessed Mia Farrow, reckons that in mid-1978 Satan thrillers have become as much a staple of the movie industry as Westerns once were. So we have Liv Ullman in *Mistress of the Devil*; Andy Warhol in *The Devil's Mistress*; Jacqueline Bisset in *The Deep*; Marvin Moore in *Shout at the Devil*. There's *Satan's Men*; *The Devil's Widow*; *The Devil's Playground*; *Devil's Rain*; and *The Redeemer—Satan's Son*. We're besieged with publicity on *The Possessed* and *The Car*—about a demon-possessed automobile. Then there's *Demon Seed* which builds its fable on: "From a computer's mind . . . and a woman's body. . . . A new generation of screen terror is born!" The Wall Street Journal, of all papers, runs a heavy editorial on these endless films, zeroing in on *Carrie*, sequel to *The Omen,* which features a possessed child, who, with supernatural intelligence, gains control of its parents—and eventually the world. It's not the grotesque or the gruesome in this evil plethora of evil films which is so frightening to a Bible believer. It's that they so exactly fit into what the prophetic Scriptures teach is in man's future. *The National Enquirer* solicits the opinion of two top psychiatrists, who state frankly that this movie movement personalizes the vast forces of evil into the human form of "The Antichrist."

Time states of Punk Rock that there is only one way to describe it: A "perversion," citing that anyone who would wear raw meat on the front of his costume is trying to do more than rebel.

Currently, the hottest commodity in England has been "The Pistols" Rock Group, who make the Beatles look like a band of angels in comparison. Their lyrics, for example, include a number entitled "Anarchy in the U. K.," which gloats blasphemously: "I am antichrist, I am an anarchist. Don't know what I want, but I know how to get it—I wanna destroy." And speaking of the Beatles, Charles Manson claims that it was while listening to the Beatles that he decided he was a christ—actually, an anti-christ. It was relevant that the *Paris Le Monde,* when Elvis Presley died, fingered him as the first "Demon of Rock." It's been downhill since.

Has Christ the answer? Yes. We read in the very first chapter of St. Mark's Gospel that "at even when the sun did set, they brought unto him [Jesus] all that were diseased and them that were possessed with devils. And all the city was gathered together at the door. And he healed many that were sick of divers diseases, and cast out many devils; and suffered not the devils to speak."

Some time ago, I ran into Colonel Sanders in Toronto airport. He, of course, was from the American Bible Belt. He was a churchgoer, on and off, all his life. He gave the world Kentucky Fried Chicken. But he was 79 years of age and not a Christian. He still belonged to the devil. So, he thought about it. He felt deep in his heart the call of Christ. He asked Jesus to come into his life. Christ did. And he testifies: "You know, it just seemed like a great burden was lifted off my shoulders. I'd never felt anything like that before, and here I was 79 years old." That, friend, is the way to deal with the devil: ask Jesus in.

Since Eve and Adam in Eden, man has morally deteriorated, due to the devil and his demonic forces, working worldwide. In 1978 Pulitzer Prize winning columnist James Reston of *The New York Times* (who confesses no particular religious faith) reckons we are living in a "moral pigsty." Exhorted Aleksandr Solzhenitsyn in his 1978 Convocation address at Harvard (which spread waves throughout the world): man today is in "a spiritualized and irreligious humanistic consciousness," besieged by sinister forces of evil, as he wallows in a sea of corruption and debilitating filth. Its source is the devil. St. Paul wrote to Timothy that in the last days man, due to "evil men and seducers shall wax worse and worse, deceiving and being deceived" (2 Tim. 3:13), for in these "latter times" society will be besieged by "seducing spirits and doctrines of devils" (1 Tim. 4:1).

A 1978 film is *Maniac: The Maniac Kills*—anywhere . . . anytime! "Their agony was his esctasy." It's like the world of Jesus' day which lived in terror of the Maniac of Gadara. The world of 1977 paid more attention to one news event than to any other: the terrorizing of 10 million New Yorkers for 12 months by the Son of Sam Killer, David Berkowitz. When caught he maintained that he took his directions directly and exactly from the devil—directions which panicked a police force larger than the whole of the national armies of 95% of the countries in the U.N. Before his sentencing he wrote: "I am really a destructive monster . . . a modern-day Judas . . . a child of Satan . . . unfit to live on this planet and breathe God's air." That's the power of the devil in one man.

Canadian papers featured the contentions of Catholic Priest Roland Joncas that Patrick McMurray, 19, strangler of a homosexual, was demon possessed. Reverend Joncas, in a seven-page affadavit to the British Columbia Supreme Court, maintained that when McMurray murdered "something grabbed him from behind on his arms and his arms burned several times hotter than touching a stove. At the same time, lights went on and off in the room rendering McMurray an evil personality."

I'm sure that demonism has a great deal to do with homosexuality—e.g., the joint killing of 28 nude males by Patrick Kearney and David Hill of Houston. The Bible condemns homosexuality and lesbianism as devilish. In West Toronto, 26-year-old Henry Williams, rapist and repeat murderer of girls, told the court that when he committed his crimes, "he was a man possessed." *Time* quotes him: It "would just be building up inside me. It was like something taking over my body, something that I couldn't control." That is the devil: no doubt about it.

Jesus assured that prior to His coming again, the earth would be "filled with violence" (Luke 17:26, Gen. 6:11, 12). Then, when Messiah comes to set up His kingdom, "violence shall no more be heard" (Isa. 60:18). Meanwhile, it could be said that "violence," as in Ezekiel's day, "filled the land" (Ezek. 8:17, 28:16). In his 1977 reception speech of the Nobel Prize, Aleksandr Solzhenitsyn lamented, "Violence, less and less restricted by the age-old legality, brazenly and victoriously strides throughout the world, unconcerned that its futility has been demonstrated and exposed by history many times." Murder in Canada has doubled in a dacade. While hardly a politician will pronounce capital punishment above a whisper, the Gallup Poll's latest reading is that 75% of the people want it back. A former, very liberal, United Church Moderator now laments: "Violent crime is growing in almost all sectors of society." Violent rape is up 13% in the U.S. in a year and 21% in Canada, despite the fact that Professor Donald Dutton, of the University of British Columbia, reckons only one rape in 10 is even reported. In the Eastern United States, I read a recent headline: "Violence by Juveniles Jumps Alarmingly." In the West: "Juvenile Crimes: Why the Sudden Rise in Violence?" *Time* describes the brutal savagery of "Youthful criminals (who) prey on the most defenseless victims. The very young, the old, the lame, the sick and blind are slugged, slashed and shot. They have retreated with broken limbs and emotional scars behind triple-locked doors." All of the polls indicate that violence on television, despite all the costly commissions, investigations and official castigations, is soaring higher than ever. Ninety-two percent of the medical doctors link it to the increase of mental illness. Crimnologists universally concur today that with a violent act every two minutes, even on children's TV, TV is spawning child criminals. Ninety percent reckon that the most potent instructor for jailed criminals is their watching crime on TV.

A front-page headliner recently said, "Criminal Behavior as Normal as Breathing." Of course! Christ said, "Out of the heart proceedeth . . . murder" (Mark 7:21-23). Professor Norman Bell recently said that the answer to crime is when "our educational system attempts to teach children there are successful ways to deal with aggressive, hateful feelings." Teaching to the head is vain without preaching to the heart. Jesus changes hearts. In Psalm 72:14, we're assured that the Lord "shall redeem their soul from deceit and violence, and precious shall their blood be in his sight." The answer to Satan is the Savior! to crime is Christ! to violence is victory in Jesus!

Russell Coyne is today a proven preacher of the gospel. According to his wife, Millie, he is "very honest, deeply religious, and a wonderful husband and father. It's a far cry from his sawed-off shotgun and knife days." What happened? Well at 11, Russell tells how he was "mean and violent. Before I knew it stealing became an obsession. . . . I graduated to . . . armed robbery." At 18 his violence and thievery had him facing a ten-year prison term. There in prison, Christ called him: "I was so very low—totally depressed. I was rotten to the core and there didn't seem to be any way out. The idea of ten long, dark years locked up in a prison really terrified me." He prayed: "Lord, I don't want to be like this. I don't want to spend the rest of my life in and out of jails. I want you to forgive my sins and come into my heart and change me. Please help me." Suddenly I felt this surge of warmth flowing through my body. It was as if something was really changing inside. It was the greatest feeling. I was filled with the power of God and I sobbed with relief. I spent my time in prison learning . . . the Bible. . . . I won parole after three years in jail and immediately I began attending church." Now like the early apostles, Russell Coyne is going everywhere preaching the Gospel.

What is opening millions up to demons, today, are drugs, a trend that escalated in the sixties. Haight-

Ashbury, Greenwich Village in New York, Yorkville in Toronto, and Soho in London were supposed to be suburbs of paradise: where the turned-on generation was. As *Time* put it, "The times were out of joint—and the young were into joints." To be in, you had to get spaced out on drugs, make obscene gestures at the establishment and a ticket into a love-in was to hate your parents. The road to paradise was to drop out, to hide behind a human hedge of hair down to your waist, front and back if possible, burn your draft card, wardrobe and push into a pair of tight jeans and wear them in perpetuity. Then you'd flop into a commune, spurn marriage, and hitchhike with Timothy O'Leary! You were into Beatlemania with the Beatles! You'd roll with the Rolling Stones, applaud Jerry Rubin, Charlie Manson and groove on Rod McKuen. You'd get caught in a coffin before you'd salute a flag, cast a vote for free enterprise over Mai Tse-Tung, Gue Grevara, Fidel Castro or Ho Chi Mingh! It was all part of the scene. President Carter laments that smoking pot is still in a "definite upward trend." Currently in New York City, 77% of the high schoolers have tried it. Eight percent are on heroin, and there are half a million heroin addicts in the United States. Here in Canada, according to *The Toronto Sun,* as many as 70% of high schoolers have fired up on pot.

The U. S. Congress stated in 1977 that for the first time, a majority (53%) of high school seniors had smoked pot. In the autumn of '77, the Canadian Federal Health Department announced that in the past year, there had been another staggering 21% increase in marijuana and hashish convictions. And in the area of hard drugs, a shocking 10 million North Americans have tried cocaine.

In the final book of the Bible, we are clearly told that whole peoples will be demonized through the use of drugs, and the result will be the climactic war of human history, Armageddon. Dudley Young has written in *The New York Times* on "the Magic of Peyote," in which he argues very convincingly the case for a link between drugs and demons.

The 1976 National Drugs Abuse Conference in New York, a U. S. Government Agency to which President Carter is personally pledged, reported its definitive examination of the various schemes for drug addicts kicking their habit: "The U.S. Government has hailed the 70% drug rehabilitation rate by Teen Challenge as the highest in the country." Commending other reformation concepts, it stressed: "The study cited Teen Challenge's 'spiritual dimension' as the key to its success." Of course, the whole basis for Teen Challenge's thrust is conversion to Christ. The Jewish psychiatrist professor, Dr. Sol Levine, of the University of Toronto, concluded in a clinical study of conversion that he had come across many speed freaks, alcoholics, druggies—suffering from everything from clinical depression to insomnia who have been really and truly cured, not by modern therapy but by religious conversion.

I was recently in the Maritines and speaking on the subject of drugs and drunkenness. A 22-year-old named Dean came into the meeting. He was captivatingly handsome, married, and had two children. But he found life too much so he had dropped out and gone into drugs. He heard Christ's call to come home, came forward and committed himself to Christ. When I talked to him afterwards, he was just bubbling with the joy of Jesus in his life.

In 1 Peter 5:7 we read of man's "adversary the devil [who], as a roaring lion, walketh about, seeking whom he may devour." St. Paul wrote to Timothy that apart from the deliverance of Christ, people find themselves inveigled into "the snare of the devil, who are taken captive by him at his will" (2 Tim. 2:26). Dr. Charles Beck of the University of Calgary sees demonism as one of the Canadian preoccupations of our time. A recent United Presbyterian Church Commission report states that modern man's efforts to eliminate the idea of a personal devil have backfired with a vengeance. They've all been "vain attempts to escape from the evil reality of man's adversary, an antiChrist devil." Anyone, it says, "who takes a long and hard look at the intractable abysmal depth of human iniquity cannot honestly deny that behind it is a monstrously wicked personality whom the Bible calls Satan." Pope Paul insisted that "whoever refuses" to acknowledge a personal devil's "existence is beyond the pale of biblical or ecclesiastical teachings."

In Revelation 20:10, we read of the devil as a deceiver; in John 13:2 as the betrayer of Jesus; in John 8:44 as a murderer and a liar; in 1 Peter 5:8 as "the adversary"; in 2 Timothy 2:26 as a snare layer; in Ephesians 6:11 of the wiles of the devil; in Acts 13:10 as the enemy of all righteousness; in Acts 10:38 as "the oppresser." Beginning at verse 10 in John 10, Jesus declared: "The thief [that is, the devil] cometh not but for to steal, and to kill, and to destroy; I am come that they might have life, and that they might have it more abundantly. I am the good shepherd: the good shepherd giveth his life for the sheep. But he that is an hireling, and not the shepherd, whose own the sheep are not, seeth the wolf coming, and leaveth the sheep, and fleeth: and the wolf catcheth them, and scattereth the sheep. The hireling fleeth, because he is a hireling, and careth not for the sheep. I am the good shepherd, and know my sheep, and am known of mine. The Father knoweth me, even so know I the Father: and I lay down my life for the sheep" (vv. 10-15).

When Jesus made unmistakably clear that the human race was in two flocks: those who followed Him and those whose god was the devil, we read that there was a division among the people. One fellowship allied themselves with Him; the other fellowship aligned with Satan. When Jesus performed miracles, those who were against Christ actually snorted: "He hath a devil"; and those who were going with Jesus reasoned: "These are not the words of him that hath a devil. Can a devil open the eyes of the blind?" Not only could He, but would He? Jesus was God—doer only of good. Satan was the devil—doer of evil! So Jesus was on earth to save; Satan, to destroy.

The Bible makes unmistakably plain that all who are not Christ's need deliverance from the devil! I recently received a letter from Carole and Bob Lux of South Bend, Indiana, where Bob is a newscaster on the CBS affiliate Radio/TV station there. Carole, a beautiful lady, had been brought up in a devil-controlled home in Detroit, where both her parents were into Spiritualism as mediums. Carole's early religion was to attend séances. Married to Bob, she suffered constant depressions, not only requiring regular therapy from a psychiatrist but all kinds of pills: pills to get to sleep, pills to wake up, pills to work, pills to relax. Then one day, one of our books fell into her hands and she longed for deliverance. After one of our TV programs, she knelt down and gave her life to Christ. Eventually, her husband, Bob, got interested and came to the Billy Graham Crusade in the great football stadium of Notre Dame and came forward to give his life to Christ. Sometime later, I received a six-page, single-spaced, type-written testimony—about the length of the book of Ephesians—telling how Carole and Bob Lux had been translated out of the Kingdom of darkness into the Kingdom of God's dear Son.

3
Superbaby

In the film *Superman*, we are presented with a world that was created good by God, but corrupted by the archvillain Luthor. Luthor's evil, however, is counteracted whenever and wherever Superman appears. Where does Superman come from? From Superbaby who descends to earth from outerspace. Who sends him? His father! It seems that Hollywood has few new ideas. In John 4:14 we read that "the Father sent the Son to be the Saviour of the world."

Man, by sin, is reduced to a beggar status. St. Paul wrote about those who turn to "the beggarly elements, where unto ye desire . . . to be in bondage?" (Gal. 4:9). There's a spiritual blindness in modern society which makes men beggars: sort of a smoggy blah that's settled in. Despite space travel, potential thermo-nuclear extinction, increase in major earthquakes, unprecedented population explosion, a famine bomb about to explode, runaway inflation and plethora of crises, modern man has slumped into a blah syndrome. We're assaulted on the one side by the politicians; and on the other, by the press. Bombarded by old man materialism and the media, advertising dulling our senses with a paradise—almost—but lost—we are told how to think, act, buy, do, smile, put our hair

—and walk. And most of us robot well! We're forced into a dry, dull mold: the Pepsi generation, pop bottle babies. We seek relief from pain—at the top from aspirin, in the middle from tums, and at the bottom from Preparation H. In between, we smother ourselves with roll-ons, spray and aerosol unguents, powders, oils and Chanel Number 5. We've got instant coffee, instant tea, instant TV meals, instant Cup-a-soup, instant divorce, instant potatoes, tomatoes and puddings. Beige is our favorite color; bland, our favorite brand. Easy credit, no-pain payments: buy now, pay later. The whole trip is so cool, smooth, soft-blah. The only problem is that it doesn't work. It's the blah—the so-what society. It's a society of beggars.

But God, as the old deists used to say, does not abandon man to his lostness. He sees man as a beggar, and He makes the Bread of Life available to him. Evangelism, says Leighton Ford, is one beggar telling another beggar where to get bread. That ancient woman of prayer, Hannah, ruminated: "The Lord . . . bringeth down to the grave and bringeth up. The Lord maketh poor, and maketh rich: He bringeth low, and lifteth up. He raiseth up the poor out of the dust, and lifteth up the beggar from the dunghill, to set them among princes, and to make them inherit the throne of glory.

Many newspapers and TV commentators believed that Jimmy Carter was doing himself harm by declaring his religiosity. They were certain he would offend vast number of voters by his openness. How little these reporters understood about the people who hungered for a man of commitment and conviction, a man who believes "that the Bible, composed of the Old and the New Testaments, is God's inspired and infalible Word, and the standard and final authority for all conduct, faith, and doctrine."

"Why Not the Best?" Jimmy Carter titled his autobiography. To Jimmy Carter the BEST can be found in the Bible.

Audrey Bonsall of Western Ontario gave her life to Christ while watching our television program Agape. Born in England, like all of us, she had all her needs met, but spiritually she was a beggar. Now, her life half over, she asked Jesus, the Bread of God sent down from heaven, to share her life. Every morning she is into her Bible for assurance, answers and direction from Christ.

Why did God love man? That is a question that must remain one of the mysteries of eternity, until such time as God himself decides to reveal it to His saints. But *that* He loved us, we can be sure. "The Lord appeared of old unto me," wrote the ancient Jeremiah (31:3), "saying, Yea, I have loved thee with an everlasting love: therefore with lovingkindness have I drawn thee." "But God commendeth his love toward us," revealed St. Paul to the Romans (5:8) "in that, while we were yet sinners, Christ died for us." It's God, not the top pop song, who truly says: "I've Already Loved You."

People today are starved for love. Dr. Karl Menninger, dean of American psychiatrists, reckons the most tragic word in society today is "unloved." He says, "Love cures people—both the ones that give it and the ones who receive it." When Pelé, the King of Soccer, was retiring in 1977, he said to his fanatical fans on television in 40 countries: "I believe love is the most important thing in the world." He then invited the 76,891 gathered in the new Giants Stadium to chant "with me, three times: love, love, love." The crowd nearly went out of control. A premier hockey coach recalls that he inspired his Philadelphia Flyers to two Stanley Cup Championships by the power of love. When Vice President Walter Mondale spoke at the funeral of fellow Minnesotan Hubert Humphrey, he explained Humphrey's greatness: "He loved everybody!"

But most people today feel "unloved." According to "As It Happened," a CBC magazine program, Barbara Hutton put out 15 million dollars to hire a "gigalo" (professional male prostitute) to make love to her for 73 days, only to end up totally disillusioned. We're informed that Rita Hayworth was a pest caller to the Beverly Hills Fire Department. She repeatedly phoned to report smoke in her residence in the wee hours of the morning, when all she wanted was someone to talk to. She felt completely unloved. Dr. Jean Kirkpatrick, founder and president of Women for Sobriety in Quakertown, Pennsylvania, reckons that millions of women turn to alcoholism to try to ease the emotional pain of disappointment in love. Betty Wylie wrote in *The Canadian* recently: "Love is much harder to find than sex." Zsa Zsa Gabor recently got serious enough to say that "many women go through life without ever really finding love." George Harrison, the Beatle, verbalized that "love is not a matter of a guy mouthing 'I love you' to a girl. Often the guy means 'I lust for you.' Real love is saying 'I love you—even if you kick me in the head and stab me in the back—I love you.' "

In man's disillusionment over love, he resorts to all kinds of weird and deviant behavior. That's what's behind the gay movement of our time. That's why rape has tripled in the seventies. That's why pre and extramarital sex is pandemic.

Man needs God's love: His pure *agape* love. A pop song goes: "Calling Dr. Love." Man wants the best in love. Gene Wilder stars in the movie, *The World's Greatest Lover*. That's nothing compared to the love of God! One of the big recent films was *Ruby*, subtitled, "A Love Affair with the Supernatural." The Bible tells us of *true* supernatural love. "Herein is love, not that we loved God, but that he loved us, and sent his Son to be the propitiation for our sins," writes the apostle John.

Dave was 18. His father lived in Independence, Missouri, his mother in Houston. But they cared for neither Dave nor each other. He was left with plenty of money but with no love. Booze, sex and athletics! He indulged to the hilt. But no love! While we were having a crusade in East Texas, one of his 'crowd' was murdered. But Dave came to the gym where we were holding the meeting. Dave came forward, and the love of God was shed abroad in his heart. That very first night he was rejoicing in a barn with some other Christians—at 1 a.m. Up blew a tornado. Dave and his friends had just left and entered the house when the whirlwind struck and collapsed the roof of the barn. Dave felt that it was a further indication of God's love.

What "Superman" presents fictionally, the Bible says factually: God the Father sent His Son to earth to effect His salvation. While at Harvard, a brilliant German student told me that a little girl near Frankfurt asked her mother: "Mom, where is God?" "Oh, God," replied her mother defensively, "is everywhere." Pursuing her mom into the kitchen, the little girl said, "But I don't want God everywhere. I want Him to be somewhere. And I want Him to be Someone!"

This is precisely why Jesus came, as God the Son to be God—to be God somewhere: Someone in man's orbit. *Oh God!* is the title of a current film doing its rounds through the world. *Time* magazine begins its review of *Oh God* by suggesting: "Look at it this way. If you were God and chose to manifest yourself on earth, wouldn't you give serious consideration to appearing as George Burns?" Whatever we may reply, God did not choose to become incarnate in an 80-year-old in tennis shoes, golf cap and windbreaker.

But how He *did* come down was in Jesus Christ His Son! Yes, it was through Christ's coming that God bore "witness, both with signs and wonders, and with divers miracles, and gifts of the Holy Ghost" (Heb. 2:4). There are some current movies entitled *Fantom From Space* and *Tony and Tia, Two Cosmic Beings—From Outer Space*. Whether phantom or fiction, these plots are only man crying out: "I want God to come down." He did!!

Only as "God come down," could Jesus cope with human need. For instance, no mere mortal could hear two prayers at once, let alone attend to the simultaneous cries of 4 billion humans. When President Carter went on the telephone in 1977 to talk one by one to the people, 9 million tried to get through to him: forty-two made it. One who didn't was a man in Tallahassee, Florida, who was buried six feet under in a cemetery, with a TV set, a CB radio and three telephones at his side. But he couldn't get through. Why? Because President Carter is a man. He can speak to everybody in general on television; but by telephone, he can speak to only one at a time. Jesus Christ is God. So He can take your call, person to person.

Whether or not Jesus Christ was God's Son is the biggest and most crucial issue ever faced by man: one which each individual must squarely confront personally, their response determining their choice of heaven or hell. Jesus said plainly to Nicodemus that it was "God" who "sent . . . his Son into the world" and consequently, "he that believeth on him is not condemned: but he that believeth not is condemned already, because he hath not believed in the name of the only begotten Son of God" (John 3:18).

The matter of the incarnation—not reincarnation—but the incarnation of God in Christ is absolutely crucial to man's hopes. St. Paul wrote, "God was in Christ, reconciling the world unto himself" (2 Cor. 5:19). The newspapers and theological journals have been full of reviews on two new controversial books in England, the one entitled *The Myth of God Incarnate,* and the extremely impressive answer: *The Truth of God Incarnate.* But this is no new, modern controversy! It is as old as man. If you're willing to recognize Christ as Lord, you'll believe He's the Son of God. If you're not, you'll try not to acknowledge that He's God the Son because to do so would be to hammer your sinful life-style. The peerless philosopher, G. K. Chesterton, reasoned with pristine clarity that the most important question you could ask about any individual is simply: "What does he believe?" Do you believe on the Lord Jesus Christ? Until and unless you do, you'll continue to hum, "I'm Always Chasing Rainbows." A pre-med student dropping acid in Denver is quoted as saying that in the last 800 years everyone has had to get high on booze, dope or the church in order to escape suicide. There was a picture of Red Skelton in the press recently with the words underneath: "Behind that clowning there's a bitter Red Skelton." Everyone Christless eventually goes bitter: if not here—then hereafter. Professor Milton Everett, of Syracuse University in New York, has spent much of a lifetime studying religious cults. He reckons 30 million North Americans have recently gone into cult movements. Why? Because it's Christ or a cult.

The vital essence of the Christian Gospel is that Christ is God incarnate. Any departure from this foundation erects a spiritual superstructure which is sitting on jelly.

There was a TV documentary recently on the life of Lenin which stated that all over the Soviet Union the school children sing, "Lenin lived, Lenin lives, Lenin will live. Lenin is everywhere." What nonsense! Lenin died in 1924. I've seen his body in a Mausoleum in Moscow. On the other hand, Jesus Christ is alive—forevermore. That's the triumph of knowing Jesus: He lived, He lives, He'll always live in His people! John Kenneth Galbraith, in his recent BBC TV documentary on Karl Marx described how the father of communism in his latter years was morose, melancholy—indeed, quite inconsolably unhappy. He overindulged food, alcohol, and tobacco, and couldn't sleep nights. He was supposedly devoted to the proletariat, but the only proletarian person he associated with closely was the woman with whom he had an illegitimate son. He died distraught and lonely. He really ceased living long before he died. He was anything but an exemplary saint!

Jesus, on the contrary, lived a perfect life—perfect in virtue and perfect in joy. Emerson once said, "Every hero becomes a bore at last." Not Jesus! Jesus came to give joy and freedom! "God lifted a heavy burden from my mind" reads a letter we received recently from a woman who had given her life to Christ. "I was trying to be saved by following the Law, but through your ministry Jesus revealed what grace and freedom through Him means. Since . . . I have led a Bible study in my own home and taught religious education in our parish." She had joy, freedom and life because Jesus was the Author of joy, freedom and life. That's why He came.

It was Christmas eve. King Gustav of Sweden saw

an unconscious girl dying in the snowbank. He laid his encumbrances aside, plunged into the snow, lifted her up and carried her into his warm palace. Christ came into this world as a man to rescue us from sin in much the same way.

Surgeon Richard Selzer writes his book on *Essays on the Art of Surgery*. He comments that people today are turning to surgeons and demanding they be their priest and savior! No! Jesus is our Great High Priest. And He is our Savior. And there is an unquenchable compulsion in all of us to feel drawn to the Cross of Christ. I'm sure this was reflected in Freddie Prinze—before he committed suicide. He insisted that all his friends watch the assassination of John Kennedy with him again and again on video tape. He had this obsession in him. When Rita Hayworth recently was deep in depression and alcoholism, she'd keep going out into her front yard to curse a tree and talk to it as if it were a person. What was this but looking for Christ, who hung on a cursed tree for the sins of me, you—and Rita Hayworth? St. Paul wrote to the Galatians (3:13), "Christ hath redeemed us from the curse of the law, being made a curse for us: for it is written, Cursed is every one that hangeth on a tree."

But we must come by faith to the cross in order to be saved. B. J. Thomas at 34 had sung to the top of the charts, the song of the decade: "Raindrops Keep Falling on My Head!" With his slightly husky Welsh tenor baritone with the South Texas accent, he sold 32 million records. Then he went through 2 million dollars en route to bankruptcy. His ride on the roller coaster began at 15 in Houston. Says B. J., "I started singing with a group when I was about 15. You kept your hair long . . . you wore a black suit and you took pills, and that went along with the mystique of being a musician. It was a romantic thing. It was an adventure.

When I was 23 I knew I was really dependent on the drugs. I was on any kind of speed I could get ahold of. Pot was a daily thing. When you get into the speed, you've got to have the barbituates to come down. . . . I was introduced to cocaine in 1968. Cocaine became my master. It was an everyday struggle to get a fix. I had a drug habit that cost me $3,000 a week. It completely ruled my life. I couldn't walk on stage, I couldn't talk on the telephone, I couldn't speak one-on-one to a person unless I was high. I (tried) withdrawal. It's a nightmare. My body went beserk. I saw monsters. . . . I blacked out. They put me in the hospital. They thought I had a brain tumor. The doctor told my wife, 'He needs a brain operation.' " But it was another kind of healing therapy B. J. Thomas needed.

He was in Los Angeles in January 1976, separated from his wife, Gloria. Gloria had a glorious conversion. One day B. J. called Gloria and she implored him to come home—sort of like his song: "Home Where I Belong." He couldn't sleep, and his drugs weren't getting him high any longer. In abject despair, he went home to Gloria. When she told him she was a Christian, he sulked for days. Then one night they were at the home of Jim Reeves, the Fort Worth cowboy, who himself had undergone a remarkable change in his life. It was Jesus. Suddenly B. J. late in the evening looked at his wife and "it was like a light that glowed around Gloria and it glowed around [the] Reeves. . . . I realized that I was at a point where I could receive the Truth. That there was a way out of what I had been in. Jim Reeves and I sat down at his dining room table. He read to me from the Bible. We prayed. Oh, it was just . . . I got up from the table and I . . . couldn't stop laughing. And he was crying. And, oh, it was a wonderful thing . . . to me it's miraculous." For B. J. Thomas, it was not a transitory experience. It was a whole new life.

He concludes, "When I accepted the Lord, when I became a born-again Christian in January of 1976, I just gave all [my habits—drugs and all] to the Lord. I said, 'Lord, I can't stop it and I just give it to You.' And I really am a miracle before man and before God because He took it from me." He has since found his niche in a happy home with Gloria and their family and he says, "As far as my Christian ministry goes, it's not in the church, between two candles! Hey, Jesus was crucified out in the garbage dump, right in the middle of the market place, and that's where God wants most of His Christians—not as a part of the world, but as a part of Christianity to be a testimony to people in this world." And that's where B. J. Thomas is today. He's been healed by the power of Christ.

4

Super Doer

Superbaby grows up into Superman and seems to be able to do anything. He can leap over skyscrapers in one gargantuan bound. He tames the bursting flood waters from a collapsing dam. He catches a crashing helicopter in midair. The people are left asking: "Is there anything too hard for Superman?"

Which, of course, takes us straight to the Bible, where the prophet Jeremiah exults: "Ah Lord God! behold, thou hast made the heavens and the earth by thy great power and stretched out arm, and there is nothing too hard for thee." God replies: "Behold I AM the Lord, the God of all flesh: is there anything too hard for me?" (Jer. 32:17, 27).

The Bible is the story of God's Son, who came, saying, "All power is given unto me in heaven and in earth" (Matt. 28:18). Today's world is intoxicated with power: nuclear power, money power, mind power, political power, personality power, horsepower, controlling power, power skating, power hitting, power steering, power brakes, power mowers.

We need to be reminded, as said the Psalmist, "God hath spoken once; twice have I heard this that power belongeth unto God" (Ps. 62:11). "All power is a trust," declared Disraeli. God the Father entrusted

His power in heaven and earth to His Son Jesus. In "Christ," wrote St. Paul to the Colossians, "dwelleth all the fulness of the Godhead bodily" (Col. 2:9). And He "is the head of all principality and power" (v. 10). This, of course, was not just when He was incarnate here on earth, but always. "Before Abraham was I AM," He said. So that when Abraham and Sarah stood before the Lord to receive instructions about the miraculous birth of Isaac, God himself asked them: "Is anything too hard for the Lord?" (Gen. 18:8). And a miraculous birth took place, which altered the whole course of history. Who was on the spot to perform the miracle? Jesus, the Son of God.

In 1978 the attention of the whole world was occupied by the first birth of a baby conceived outside the womb of a woman. On July 25th, Leslie Brown of Oldham, England, gave birth to baby Louise Brown. It was made possible as a result of the long-term research of British gynecologist, Patrick Steptoe, and Cambridge physiologist, Robert Edwards. In a test tube they combined the sperm of John Brown with an ovum from Leslie Brown, and implanted the tiny fetus in the womb of the mother. She carried the baby until nine days previous to its expectant birth date, and a Caesarian section brought little Louise into the world.

The populations of all countries immediately reacted. The British Medical Association's central ethics committee secretary, Dr. John Dawson, extolled: "I think it's a miracle of modern science." British Member of Parliament, Leo Abse, scolded: "The test-tube baby could be the first step toward the creation of a Hitler-style master race . . . genetic engineering now has come to such a perilous course that a Dictatorship could create a master race." Everywhere voices were lamenting that Aldous Huxley's *Brave New World* or Orson Welles' *Big Brother: 1984* were about to appear. Few remained mute on the issue.

Even the church was sharply divided. The Roman Catholic Bishop of Middlesborough snapped that the technique for Louise Brown's birth was definitely unlawful, while the Church of England's theologian, Professor Robert Berry, spoke for the Anglicans: "I can see nothing theologically wrong with it." The objections centered on the ominous spectre of "master races," motherhood for hire, and "armies of clones."

Cloning also got worldwide publicity in 1978 with the publishing of David Rorvik's *In His Image: Cloning of a Man*. The claim of the book—generally thought to be fallacious—is that there existed a 14-month-old boy who had been "cloned" from the cell of a wealthy, unidentified, unmarried man.

In addition to the cloning concept—which geneticists are saying is definitely possible—there is artificial insemination. Perhaps the most publicized baby born by this technique was that of a world noted lady cartoonist who gave birth in 1978 to a baby born as a result of her late husband's sperm being implanted in her womb six months after his death. (The sperm had been frozen.) When the baby was born, the father had been dead sixteen months.

Let's sum up how humans have arrived on the planet earth. The first birth was the most remarkable. Adam came into being with neither mother nor father. Eve arrived without a woman. Jesus made His entrance without a man. And now we have babies from artificial insemination, a baby conceived in a test tube, and perhaps a cloned baby.

Who made all of this possible? Christ the Son of God, the origin and orderer and orchestrator of all life! "In him was life, and the life was the light of men" (John 1:4), wrote St. John after explaining: "All things were made by him, and without him was not anything made that was made" (John 1:3).

Some of us will never forget when Frank Borman, as the first modern man in moon orbit to speak to men on earth, read from the opening verses of the Bible: "In the beginning God created the heaven and the earth." But Borman saw only the inner edge of outer space. Today, not even the most sophisticated, two-mile-long electric telescopes can give man a view of a solitary planet outside the solar system. Stars, yes; planets, no! Whole pages in newspapers currently are advertising the June 1979 release of the film, *Outer Space Is Not Empty*. It isn't! In John 1:3, we read that all things were made by him [Jesus]; and without him was not anything made that was made."

In mid-1978, I was addressing a gathering of students in St. John, New Brunswick. At the end someone told me about Denis, who had received his Bachelor's Degree from McGill and his Master's in Science from Cornell. He was an agnostic because he couldn't understand the origin of the universe. On our television program, "Agape," one Sunday afternoon, we were dealing with the theme of Christ's coming from the highest heaven to the lowest death on earth in order that He might save us. We asserted that, had there been only one inhabitant of earth, Christ would have come and died for him. The consequence was that Denis got down on his knees and gave his life totally to Christ, and is today studying for the ministry.

Christ can do anything! In the film, Superman is pictured taming the bursting flood waters from a collapsing dam. This is a vivid reminder of how Christ actually stopped the storm on tempestuous Galilee. We read in Mark 4:37-39: "And there arose a great storm of wind, and the waves beat into the ship, so that it was now full. And he [Jesus] was in the hinder part of the ship, asleep on a pillow: and they awake him, and say unto him, Master, carest thou not that we perish? And he arose, and rebuked the wind, and said unto the sea, Peace, be still. And the wind ceased, and there was a great calm." (41) "And they feared exceedingly, and said one to another, What manner of man is this, that even the wind and the sea obey him?"

He also controlled gravity. We read in Luke 4:28-30: "And all they in the synagogue, when they heard these things, were filled with wrath, and rose up, and thrust him out of the city, and led him unto the brow of the hill whereon their city was built, that they might cast him down headlong. But he, passing through the midst of them, went his way."

So Jesus could walk over hills or mountains at will, calm stormy waters, and save a sinking ship in mid-sea. Superman's feats of leaping over a skyscraper, calming a bursting dam and catching a crashing helicopter were topped by Jesus centuries ago!

Man's power sources are running out of gas these days. We've painted ourselves into a corner in our use and quest for energy power. "Energy shortage," indicates the Ann Lander's column, is currently man's greatest concern. President Carter claims the energy crisis in the U.S. is a national catastrophe. We've consumed more energy since World War II than the human race in all history prior to that time. Now we're asking: Can atomic power replace our passion to strip the world of its traditional fuels? Or are the risks too great? How about power from the sun reflected back to earth from colossal mirror-like satellites placed in earth's orbit? How about windmills, a million times bigger than we had back on our Saskatchewan farm, to pump water—or to generate electricity? How about tidal power harnessing the ocean tide sweeping in and out of the Bay of Funday? Where are we going to get power? I don't know. I'll leave those crises to others.

But when it comes to spiritual power, Jesus promised before His ascension that we can "receive power after that the Holy Ghost is come upon" us. And that's how He will release His miracle-working power to us today.

St. Augustine, 1500 years ago, explained: "Miracles do not happen in contradiction to nature but only in contradiction to that which is known to us of nature." Jesus Christ today performs miracles on man's behalf just as He always has. David R. Hayes was writing recently about how monumental the problems are today. It seems that being a brilliant "intellectual" or a leader with abundant "charisma" is simply not enough. Perhaps we need a want ad displayed to outer space which states: "Miracle worker required." Mr. Hayes, that Person is already among us!

The United Church of Canada in its 27th General Council, in August, 1977, affirms the verity of "the New Testament . . . healing miracles" of Jesus. It points out that there are at least 24 accounts of healing miracles in the Gospels. It stresses in this officially adopted report, called "The Lordship of Christ," that God "reaches out to our whole being, seeking that healing / health / salvation which makes us whole."

We were holding an Easter Crusade with 50 or 60 churches in California in 1978. It was adjacent to Travis Airforce Base in California. I preached in the chapel service there on Sunday morning. That night in the gymnasium that Airforce head, with his family, was in the second row from the front. I was telling how Christ wanted to take charge of every life. The Commander came forward with members of his family to enthrone Christ in his life. He had had a recent brush with death. He was aboard the largest airplane ever to fly—the C5—coming in from the Pacific. As they made the approach for a landing the wheels jammed. They circled four hours. They refueled in the air. Finally they came down after all the preparations had been made for a crash landing. The great man was unhurt, but he was also resolved to give his whole life to Christ. Easter Sunday night, 1978, he settled it. Since that night he has been opening his staff meetings in prayer, because God is the new Ruler of his life.

Christ can do anything in nature and in human events. A Cabinet member of the Federal Government recently avowed that it would take a superman to solve today's gigantic problems. Well, we've got Jesus Christ! Daniel Friberg writes that this is "an age when more and more people appear either beset by total despair for the future or have hope only in the supernatural." The Christian is in the hands of the supernatural Christ. The ancient St. Paul wrote to the Philippians: "I can do all things through Christ which strengtheneth me."

The May, 1978, number of Yale University's *Daily News Magazine* revealed that it had sent out over 160 inquiries to writers, athletes, artists, actors and politicians to discover if they had fears. Muhammed Ali said he feared flying. John Wayne feared the things fire, wind and water can do when nature reverses itself. Barbara Walters was afraid of violence, kidnapping, and being misquoted. Charles Colson reported that he had no fears, other than the fear of God, "not because of my strength, but rather the strength each of us can receive from the Lord Jesus Christ." I saw the Reimer Express ad recently on TV: "We've got what it takes to take what you've got!" Christ has what it takes to take what you've got.

To be without Christ is to be without hope. In late

1978, *Time* magazine described a novelist who had died as the "most famous writer in the world. Eighty million copies of his books had been sold, his plays were performed worldwide, his work had led to several memorable movies, and some 80 of his short stories had been adapted for television. At his famous Villa Mauresque, he employed one of the best cooks on the Riviera, dined off silver plates and entertained royalty. Yet he was miserable." What was wrong with Somerset Maugham? Everything, he said as he grieved, "My success means nothing to me." In one of his nearly innumerable cries of anguish he lamented, "All I can think of now are my mistakes. I can think of nothing else but my foolishness. . . . I wish I'd never written a single word. It's brought me nothing but misery."

Richard Nixon, in his David Frost interviews, said that the deadest, most bored people on earth are the wealthy pleasure-seekers, lolling in the glamorous watering places of the South of France or the East Coast of Florida, going from golf course to cocktail party to bridge set, without ever having found a reason for living. Some of us feel very sorry for Princess Margaret, sunk into years of deep, sometimes manic, depression. We grieve for Margaret Trudeau who was thrust into "shaking hands and smiling in crowded halls." "I'm tired of that sort of thing," she wailed. Teenage Manitobans Kimberly Werzonski and Donna Werbitski pleased the Dental Association for smiling non-stop for 28 hours. But you can have a smile on the outside while you've bile in your belly, guile in your heart, and strife in your psyche. Comedian Shecky Green laments: "I'd like my obituary to read, 'He lived once and once was enough.' I hope there is no reincarnation. I don't want to go through all that again." "It was hell," the Captain and Tennille now say of their television program. Clint Eastwood laments: "I sometimes think I've been working all my life to be 'not famous.' I don't seem to have the gift it takes to enjoy fame." Sometimes I wonder: apart from Christ, does anyone? Canadian-born American, Saul Bellow, won the Nobel Prize. Alas, his books portray man as frightened and alienated, striving "to find a foothold in a tottering world." A frustrated Paul Newman brushes off the plaudits and talks of his own disillusionment: "I'm just not happy. I don't have inner serenity. And I don't have the guts to do anything else." "Every day the world rolls over on someone who yesterday was sitting on it," observes Stephan Brown.

Who can turn the world right-side-up again? Those who are Christ's! In Acts 17:6, we read that outsiders reckoned that Christians were those that "have turned the world upside down."

Christ can still turn people upside down and set them right-side-up. Many of us on the Billy Graham team grieved deeply when Ethel Waters, at 80, went to be with Christ. We missed her deeply. Ethel was born after her 12-year-old mother was raped in a rat-infested, bed-bug-plagued shanty, in a redlight district of a wretched slum. As a child she was never cuddled or kissed. She slept on the floor, or at best in a rickety chair. She collected pennies by running errands for pimps, and knew the whole prostitute business by the time she was 7. At 13, she was forced into a marriage that wouldn't work, so she took off for Honkey Tonk Town and emerged as the first belter of St. Louis blues. Yes, she became the most famous and beloved female singer/actress of her time, but inside she was still blue.

Then in 1956, her life three quarters over, she came to Madison Square Garden in New York, where Billy Graham was presenting Christ. She took her stand for

Christ. She spent the rest of her days singing: "Where Jesus Is, It's Heaven There!" "His Eye Is on the Sparrow!" "Oh, How I Love Jesus!" and "Cabin in the Sky!" In her famous line, she herself was proof superb that "God don't sponsor no flops!" Christ had turned her right-side-up!

Christ has power over all men, saints or sinners. When Pilate threatened Jesus with the intimidation, "Knowest thou not that I have power to crucify thee, and have power to release thee?" Jesus answered, "Thou couldest have no power at all against me, except it were given thee from above" (John 19:10, 11). In Revelation 5:13 we read of the ascended Christ who sits upon His eternal throne: "Blessing, and honor and glory, and power, be unto him that sitteth upon the throne, and unto the Lamb for ever and ever." People who challenge this omnipotent power of Christ do so to their own peril.

I am convinced that the most universally administered judgment of God on our times is nonfulfillment. The Bible calls Jesus the true "desire of all peoples" (Hag. 2:7). As Tolstoy, the Russian, reiterated, He is the only one capable of filling man's "God-shaped blank." A letter to Ann Landers from Marge points up this truth: "I'm 44, husband same age (swell guy). We get along OK—no drinking, no gambling, no skirt chasing. He has a good job and our home is paid for.

"Our four children are healthy and normal. They do well in school and the three older ones (teenagers) have never caused us any trouble.

"So why am I writing? Because my life is blah. Something is missing. It's like stew without salt. I feel a certain emptiness. What is it?"

Psychiatrist Helen DeResis claims that 8 out of 10 women suffer from time to time from this depression syndrome: this emptiness.

Milton Berle has made the world laugh for half a century, but now confesses he can't find it in himself to be able to laugh for himself. Having gambled three and a half million dollars away, he groans that life simply has had no fun for him. Mark Rutherford wrote of "the folly which deludes us all through life with endless expectation and leaves us at death without the thorough enjoyment of a single hour." Loretta Lynn cries of how she's grabbed for success and happiness. Instead: "Deep down I'm bitter." Author George Plimpton has been out of Harvard thirty years. In addressing the senior class he strangely implored: "You who are about to enter the real world; don't go. Stop. Go back to your rooms. Unpack. Settle in. There's not much out there."

I think this spiritual balking, this raging restlessness is part of the reason that 25% of Canadians move every year. I remember on the farm in Saskatchewan, we had a lovable collie called Brownie. When one of the neighbors came by in a Model A Ford on the dirt road to Pangman, Brownie would bark like crazy and snap and grab at those left rear tires. But he never grabbed hold. I used to wonder what would happen if he had grabbed hold. It would twist his head off. But he never did. I see people in life trying so hard to grab hold. But they can't. In life, they never get there! But where's "there"? Nowhere—without Jesus. North American women use 110,000 tons of make-up per year to try and make it. It's all a nowhere trip. It's why Mick Jagger talked contemptuously of the very "rock and roll music" he belted out. It's a "dead end." Gregory Herbert, at 31, lead saxophonist of the "Blood, Sweat and Tears" group went further. He literally hit "dead end" by killing himself with an overdose in Amsterdam. And 31-year-old Terry Keith, lead guitarist with Chicago, drove a bullet through his head.

Some are trying desperately to bypass the Gospel by going on pills. Drugs is the new drunkenness—the new escape from reality in quest of Aldous Huxley's *Brave New World.*

"You name the psychic state you want and I can put you there," said Dr. Arnold Mandell, chairman of the psychiatry department at the University of California, San Diego.

"Research on psychotropic (mood-altering) drugs has advanced so far that Dr. William Bunney of the National Institute of Mental Health can say, "The Brave New World is something that's subtly and slowly emerging. We're already into aspects of it. We now have ways to alleviate distress with drugs that have specific effects on brain functioning."

What are those effects? Dr. Nathan Kline, a New York psychiatrist, sees vast possibilities: Drugs to expand the childhood sense of curiosity and learning and cut short the turbulence of adolescence; drugs to provoke or relieve guilt; drugs to deepen our awareness of beauty and our sense of awe.

More broadly, Mandell says, "The equivalent of religion and political systems is tied up in these drugs. We're talking about a real threat to the herd. We're not that far off from having someone say, "This is a place that feels good to me and, presto! one pill and he's there." But once again the question is: "Where's 'there'?"

Leighton Ford was in the Pacific Coliseum in Vancouver one night when his counseling chairman failed to arrive on time for the Reachout meeting. So they paused and prayed for him. Where was he? He was held up in the traffic. The jam was because a man, for whom modern life was simply too much, had climbed to the 12th floor of a conspicuous building and in full sight of the assembling crowd was about to jump. The counseling chairman pulled his car to the curb, scaled the stairs, and talked the man into coming off the ledge. Then he led him to Christ, and today that man is a son of God and servant of Jesus.

Finally, Jesus the Son of God can do anything for His own. St. Paul, the aged, recollected that at the beginning of his Christian experience "no man stood with me, but all men forsook me.... Notwithstanding the Lord stood with me, and strengthened me, ... and I was delivered out of the mouth of the lion. And the Lord shall deliver me from every evil work, and will preserve me unto his heavenly kingdom: to whom be glory for ever and ever. Amen" (2 Tim. 4:17, 18).

Recently on one of our Canadian television programs Marian Parkinson, a veteran missionary, appeared and told her story. When she first went overseas the ship she was on went down in the Atlantic. It was about 2 a.m. when she was obliged to plunge into the high seas. After going down twice she surfaced and saw a bright light and heard a voice saying: "Swift, go swift for the lifeboat." She saw the craft only yards away. As she floundered in the water, trying desperately to swim, she felt hands propelling her out of the water into the lifeboat.

Often, of course, the testimony of Christ is more effective in troubles than in deliverance from them. St. Paul wrote to Timothy that "all that will live godly in Christ Jesus shall suffer persecution" (2 Tim. 3:12), and to the Philippians (1:29), "For unto you it is given in the behalf of Christ, not only to believe on him, but also to suffer for his sake."

Early in 1978 I conducted crusades and conferences in Brazil. While there I had fellowship with the oldest active missionary in the world. The Reverend Harold Cook had just celebrated his hundredth birthday and was still going strong. He had preached in 740 cities and towns, beginning in 1894. His story of hardship and persecution and triumph through trials was one I shall never forget. He was, to me, the living epitome of Jesus' commissioning: "Go ye therefore . . . and lo, I am with you always, even unto the end of the world" (Matt. 28:19, 20).

Think of the people of Guatemala who suffered that terrible earthquake in 1976 which killed 23,000, injured 77,000, and destroyed 254,000 homes. Did that tragedy drive people from their faith in Christ? No! It has been estimated that there are twice as many born-again believers in Christ today throughout Guatemala as there were previous to the earthquakes.

Is Christ still our powerful "Superman" when death comes? Yes, indeed! In Revelation 1:17, 18 we read of Jesus telling the exiled apostle John, "Fear not; I AM the first and the last: I AM he that liveth, and was dead; and, behold, I AM alive for evermore, Amen; and have the keys of hell and of death." St. John was aged. Already he had gone through the fires of near-death for Christ. Where was Christ when the British family of missionary McCanns were violently slaughtered in Rhodesia in 1978? Right there with them, enabling them to endure it nobly. Where was Jesus when a third of a million Christians are slaughtered in Uganda by Idi Amin? And a comparable number in Cambodia? Jesus is right there, blessing them in death with much greater unction than they'd known in life.

5

Super Lover

"One thing *Superman* does not have—as far as anyone with plain old 20-20 can see anyway—is many laughs. Director Donner, convinced that it was campiness that brought down King Kong," strove to avoid "the possibility of untoward giggles." So commented *Time* magazine. Unlike the *Star War* characters, and nearly all modern fictionalized messiah figures, Superman is not a fun person abounding in wit, wisecracks and buffoonery. He was not Erma Bombeck, come to write a best-seller 'Life Is a Bowl of Cherries.' He was not Santa Claus, riding in a one-horse sled to the tune of jingle bells. He is a sober, serious character whose creators have obviously striven diligently to depict him as boundless in compassion and devoid of displays of ego-tripping exhibitionism. Superman is character-cast to come off as a being of essential humility and humanity, not humor.

Perhaps no character trait was more evident in the life of Jesus than His compassion. So serious was He about His mission that we never once read that "Jesus laughed!" We only read that "Jesus wept!" Had Jesus been one of those modern messiahs, He might have jauntily tripped up to Lazarus' grave with a wink and wowed the crowd as much by His care-free nonchalance as by miracle-working power. But that was not Jesus. He wept because He knew the heartbreak of the bereaved. And He himself was moved solemnly by the stark gravity and reality of grim death. It was in keeping with His being. He wept over Jerusalem. He wept over the woes of society. He was "the Man of Sorrows and acquainted with grief" (Isa. 53:3).

The New Testament word "compassion" means "passion"—to suffer: and "come"—with: "to suffer with:" or literally: "suffering with another." Jesus simply could not look at need and not be moved with compassion. For example, when the crowd was hungry, we read that Jesus deliberately said: "I have compassion on the multitude, because they have now been with me three days, and have nothing to eat: and if I send them away fasting to their own houses, they will faint by the way: for divers of them came from far" (Mark 8:2, 3).

When Jesus encountered a man reeking with leprosy, rather than turning up His nose and turning His back He "put forth his hand, and touched him, and saith . . . be thou clean" (Mark 1:41). He touched others in healing, because He himself was so touched with their needs.

Jesus is as contemporary to our times as He was to those when He was here on earth. There were the racial and ethnic barriers. Jesus told a beautiful story of a travelling man attacked, assaulted, robbed and dumped unconscious in the ditch to die unnoticed. Then a "certain Samaritan, as he journeyed, came where he was: and when he saw him, he had compassion on him" (Luke 10:33). Jesus loved through all barriers. He loved the deranged. There was that maniac of Gadara whom He confronted in the cemetery. He cast out a whole legion of demons and urged him to: "Go home to thy friends, and tell them how great things the Lord hath done for thee, and hath had compassion on thee" (Mark 5:19). The biggest thing in Jesus' miraculous transformation of this hopeless madman was that He "had compassion" on him.

And there was the father, whose son was a demoniac. The young man would throw himself into the water and into the fire in attempts to do himself in. "Have compassion on us, and help us" (Mark 9:22), pled the father. And Jesus promptly exorcised the son of the demons which possessed him. The father was ecstatic with delight. Jesus approached Nain and "there was a dead man carried out, the only son of his mother, and she was a widow. . . . When the Lord saw her, he had compassion on her and said unto her, Weep not . . . and touched the bier and . . . said, Young man, I say unto thee, Arise. And he that was dead sat up, and began to speak. And he delivered him to his mother" (Luke 7:12-15). Because Jesus would die, the dead could rise to life. Because Jesus wept, weeping people could cease their crying. A country Western is entitled "9,999,999 Tears." Jesus can dry 9,999,999 tears. John Locke, the political philosopher who, more than any other, gave birth to the American Republic, once said: "You bore deeply enough into the earth and you'll strike water. You bore deeply enough into the human heart and you'll strike tears." Only Jesus can wipe away all tears from our eyes.

With Jesus, compassion was integral to His person. When blind people had exhausted every other source of help, they had not yet read the bottom line until they had met with Jesus, who had "compassion on them, and touched their eyes."

The most conspicuous point in the most familiar story ever told, the Prodigal Son, is that when the prodigal came home, the "Father saw him and had compassion" (Luke 15:20). It was this compassion which impelled the father to run to him, embrace him, kiss him, forgive him totally; to reinstate him as his son, robe him in the best, put a gleaming ring on his hand and shoes on his feet; to kill the fatted calf and call in the whole neighborhood for a homecoming celebration.

The recounting of the Prodigal Son is a part of Jesus' trilogy of parables in which He demonstrates the compassion of a father for a lost son, the concern of a shepherd for a lost sheep, and the diligent quest of a woman for a lost coin. Four chapters hence, Luke the physician (any doctor must have compassion or be no doctor) notes how Jesus—with perhaps four or five thousand people trailing Him—stops under a sycamore tree and commands Zacchaeus to come down and He'll go home with him and save him. Why? Because "the Son of Man is come to seek and to save that which was lost" (Luke 19:10).

Ours, as a magazine cover story expresses it, is "The Lost Generation." As I write I'm looking at a headline: "Suicides in Metro [Toronto] Are Up Fourteen Percent, Poison Preferred, Coroner Says." I see another headline: "Grad Shoots Himself." It tells of a Weymouth, Massachusetts, senior, who got up to give his graduation address before the convocation of faculty, fellow students, parents and friends in the assembly hall and exclaimed, "This is the American way" and shot himself.

The late billionaire J. Paul Getty's legal advisor, Robina Lund, went public recently with the curious revelation that Getty became so lonely and psychotic that late in life he believed passionately that he was the re-incarnation of the Roman Emporer Hadrian. Though he never finished it he spent twenty-seven million dollars on a Roman Villa on a hill in Malibu, overlooking the Pacific, just to house who he thought he was. Jackson Stenner, president of the American National Testing Service, reveals that 28% of first-grade children wish they were someone else.

"Where Do You Go to Lose a Heartache?" asks the country western. Some reach for a drug. Others get drunk. Still others spend thousands on therapy. Robert Frost noted that countless souls look back only at failure, and forward only at hopelessness.

Secularists today are urging a societal compassion: the kind that used to prevail in our communities. A University of Toronto professor, John Gandy, is exhorting that we should together be looking out for the despairs of "the frail, elderly, and mentally and physically handicapped" and welcome back "into the community, patients returning from mental hospitals and inmates from prisons and correctional centers."

"The Broken Heart" used to be a religio-hill-billy phrase. But not today. Dr. James T. Lynch has published his widely quoted: *The Broken Heart: The Medical Consequences of Loneliness.* Professor of Psychology and Chief of Psychosomatic Illness Clinics at the University of Maryland, Lynch maintains loneliness, leading to broken hearts, is one of society's most devastating killers. He illustrates by pointing to "statistics that point to the fact that consistently these diseases kill between two and ten times more single people than married people." Lynch explains that "loneliness cannot be observed in a test tube. It is subjective and runs on a continuum from complete isolation to periodic feelings of friendlessness. Among the loneliest people in society are children, although we tend to equate loneliness with the aged. The number of children caught in divorces has tripled in the past two decades, there are fewer siblings in households and more mothers have joined the labor force, all of which establish an environment of 'chronic loneliness' in children. What goes on in childhood is linked to adult disease," he adds, "and children's loneliness today will express itself in disease in thirty to forty years. Then it's called heart disease!" he says.

One of Lynch's main premises is that we must attack "the myth that we're machines." Careful diets and exercise are important, he says, "but relationships are far more important than physical factors. I wrote this book to warn people of the serious consequences of loneliness in this country. I see lonely people running around parks. They have bought the idea that they're machines. Medicine cannot solve the problems caused by disruptive human relationships," he insists. "Yet we continue to pour money into medical treatments for problems caused by loneliness. No one wants to be sick. No one wants to be lonely. How are we getting boxed in?" Lynch asks. "I don't have six prescriptions for loneliness," he admits, but he calls for recognition of what he refers to as the fact that loneliness will lead to human extinction if it's not faced and solved.

Too often the broken heart, the unloved loner, the isolated, uncared for recluse is someone who is spiritually lost and alienated and feels no sense of identity. So what can that person do? Come to Jesus who truly had "compassion on the ignorant, and on them that are out of the way" (Heb. 5:2). Jesus is "The Way" (John 14:6). St. Augustine once said that he had read remarkable things in Plato, Socrates and Aristotle, but never: "Come unto me, all ye that labor and are heavy laden, and I will give you rest" (Matt. 11:28-29). Only Jesus could say that.

I was preaching for Dr. William Calderwood, my brother-in-law, in the First United Church of Lethbridge, Alberta, in 1978. Afterwards I was shaking hands at the door. A lovely lady, called Shirley, came by. Two years previous she had been a provided for wife of a rancher, and mother of three beautiful children, but one day suddenly, tragically, her husband had been killed. For three months she had struggled with loneliness and frustration, and was on the verge of despair. Then she saw our television program, "Agape," and Evie Tornquist sing "Broken Up People," and I spoke on Christ's healing of the broken heart. Shirley then and there opened herself up to Christ and, yes, He healed her broken heart! The loneliness was gone. And He gave her a new husband.

Christ has special compassion for a family. He, despite the objections of His disciples, took little children up into His arms and blessed them. His first recorded miracle was performed at the wedding in Cana of Galilee. When He hung on the cross and saw His mother desolate and alone, He ordered John to take her home and care for her. "Thus saith the Lord," we read in Jeremiah, I will "be the God of all the families" (Jer. 31:1) and again "God setteth the solitary in families." God gave Adam, Eve, observing that it was not good that man should be alone.

According to *Time,* by mid-1978, there is "one divorce for every two marriages in the U.S." Today we're seeing the nuclearization of families. Housing authorities have witnessed the average household unit shrink from six or eight down to two or three. Divorce on its own, according to a New York firm, will increase housing costs 1.2 trillion dollars in the U.S. over the next decade. Even now, the U.S. Census Bureau announces that over half of U.S. households only have one or two persons. The kids move off early and often shack up anywhere with nearly anyone, as though moral values were meaningless and as though there were no tomorrow.

Dr. Ben Schlesinger, professor of Sociology at the University of Toronto, reckons that 25% of the students at that institution are living with someone, most without any intention of being married. For many couples, Schlesinger says, it's become a game, except that when it breaks up it hurts more than many people think it will. Of course this is not just a university trend. The U.S. Census Bureau reckons that currently 1,300,000 couples have taken up living together, a fivefold increase in the seventies. What's the description used for these partners? Such new words as cohabs, inamorata, significant other, fiancee, or just plain old boyfriend or girlfriend. Certainly the standard setters, such as Hollywood, TV playwrights and personalities, are not helping repair the current disintegration of the family. Jacqueline Bisset, single at 32, stars in *The Deep* and is up there in front of the kids constantly. She says she has no intention of getting married. Her suxual relationships come and go according to her whims: "What comes first in my relationship with a man is lust. Then more lust. Then liking. Then fondness and finally love, which really means making a decision. And the only thing I have decided at the moment is that I don't want to get married." People hear Rex Harrison, at 68, say: "I don't want to get married again, but I would like to have a woman in my life." That has become a norm rather than an exception in modern life.

The late Bing Crosby, the year of his death, was asked his assessment of the disintegration of the modern home. He said he wondered what chance the kids have these days. It used to be that parents would "inculcate some goals, some values in a child." Now they just get stuck in front of a TV set, and what do they see? "Well, one afternoon, I saw a panel show, a very popular program," remonstrated Crosby. "Five women were on, all big names from films and the stage. And all five of these successful, attractive women were advocating that people live together before they get married. So a teenage girl watching these important women, these stars, is going to start thinking this is really the chic thing to do. She may move in with some guy and the first thing you know, he's got her pregnant. They have an illegitimate child, and there goes the family. Oh, they may stay together for a year or two, but, eventually," Mr. Crosby reckoned, they're nearly sure to "come apart."

Today's young, at 18, have spent 17,000 hours in front of a TV, while they've been in school 11,000 hours. What do they learn at school, all too often, these days? Kathleen Gow in *The Canadian* magazine tells us: "A teacher friend of mine tells me that one of her colleagues who teaches health shows a series of 17 slides to a mixed class of Grade 9's. The slides depict 17 positions of intercourse. A Family Life education kit at another school, having official school board approval, recommends as a sample learning experience for Grade 7's: 'Analyze the following list, differentiating the effect of each on the sex drive of the male and female: touch, smell, sight, personality, pornography, alcohol.' At yet another school, a school trustee tells me that he found a book called *Going Down With Janis* in a junior high school library: the story of Janis Joplin written (as noted on the cover) 'by her female lover.' By the example of a heroine it was a recommendation for lesbianism. The alarmed trustee took it to the police morality squad who told him if the book were selling in a bookstore, they'd raid the place." The man complained that the emphasis in today's world of romance is as often guys with gays, as guys with gals.

So what happens? The young grow up too often without moral standards at all. Clare Booth Luce, among the most influential female Americans of this century, reckons: "What we call the New Morality is actually the old immorality of decadent civilizations. And history shows that whenever the old immorality prevailed, the family was weakened and the society collapsed. If the family is indeed the basic unit of civilized society then one thing can be done: every mother and father must try to be a moral person in the traditional sense of the word. Every parent must practice and teach morality within the family. If they do, America won't go down the drain. If they don't, America will have lost its heart and soul."

A leading researcher reckons that by the eighties, 40% of all marriages will end in divorce. In 1977 there were six times as many divorce petitions filed in Canada as in 1967. And our statisticians tell us that one in four marriages in Canada today ends in divorce, and with urbanization on the increase we'll soon match the Americans. Nor does our society cry about it. Instead, it gloats—nearly glories—in the shame of our sins. Zsa Zsa Gabor is asked how she wants to be remembered. Her reply: "Just as an intelligent, beautiful actress and a wonderful wife, wife, wife, wife, wife, wife, wife!" The three Gabor sisters have been married an aggregate of eighteen times.

The people who have to deal with our disintegrating homes don't laugh about it. "Dear Abby," in an interview recently, reckoned: "Marriage is under severe attack from group sex, switching and plain old-fashioned playing around. Horrifying!" is how she describes it. Her twin sister, Ann Landers, claims that from her mail 52% of those who are married think they are married to the wrong person. So that both our present preparation for marriage and preservation of the marriage state are tragically left begging.

It seems most politicians these days support "Divorce on Demand or No Fault Divorce." They try to ignore the Catholic Bishops' objections, or the Bible-believing Protestants throughout North America. According to the National Statistical Institute, 87% of all divorces stem from adultery. This reality gets very little attention. To ignore this fact and talk about incompatibility or mental cruelty is to skirt the real issue and to ignore what the Bible says. I believe that tens of millions admired President Carter's courage when he urged: "We need a stable family life to make us better servants of the people. . . . So those of you who are living in sin, I hope you'll get married. Those of you who've left spouses, go back home, and those of you who don't remember your children's names, get acquainted." I'd like to stress that regardless of the Nicholas Von Hoffmans calling him a "born-again fundamentalist pope," our society knows that in this the President is right. An English doctor on a network talk show was asked how he'd react if he heard President Carter was having an affair. He replied: "I'd cry!"

Jesus said: "Out of the heart proceed evil thoughts . . . adulteries, fornications" (Matt. 15:19). St. Jude writes of whole "cities giving themselves over to fornication" (Jude 7). St. Paul wrote to the Ephesians (5:3): "Fornication . . . let it not be once named among you"; to the Thessalonians: It is the "will of God that ye abstain from fornication." So, Paul urged: "Flee fornication. Every sin that a man doeth is without the body; but he that committeth fornication sinneth against his own body" (1 Cor. 6:18). Jesus said plainly that "fornication" breaks up the home (Matt. 5:32), and again, "Whosoever shall put away his wife, except it be for fornication, and shall marry another, committeth adultery, and whoso marrieth her that is put away doth commit adultery."

Two families were in the Canadian national news recently, the one as a tragic failure and the other as an exemplary success. They were both sir-named Ellis. There were the Brooks Ellises of Nova Scotia and Toronto. Twenty-nine-year-old Deborah Ellis had, in fourteen years, given birth to five babies to some three fathers, three of the children tragically dead from parental negligence and cruelty and the other two taken over by the Children's Aid Society. This all cost the Canadian taxpayers 2 million dollars and was a classic example of the disaster of irresponsible womanhood, manhood, and parenthood.

The other Ellis family, of course, is the Ron Ellises. Ron was a star with the Toronto Maple Leafs in the sixties, when the Leafs were winning Stanley Cups. He was right winger on the number one line when Team Canada defeated the Russians in 1972, in the greatest hockey series ever. And he came out of retirement in 1977 to become what George Gross called Canada's best performer in the world championship tournament in Vienna. Ron Ellis has become a strong Christian and wants the whole world to know it. His marriage and family is a beautiful one, exemplary to all Canadians. In Ron's words: Three years "ago my life wasn't complete. I was searching and trying to get a real line on my life and determine just what direction I wanted to go. A Bible was presented to me and I began to take it on road trips with me. At first I started to read it when my roommate wasn't in the room, and everytime he came in I'd put it away. Eventually I started to read it all the time and realized that to fulfill what I was trying to find, I had to make a commitment. It was shortly after that, both my wife and I asked the Lord to come into our lives and I really feel that I have found out what life is all about."

The Ron Ellises were once in a *dilemma* about life—about marriage, about their family, about parenthood. No more! True love is the answer to our home problem. Love, not lust, needs to be the basis for a romance. In Genesis 29:18, 20, we read: "And Jacob loved Rachel; and said [to her father Laban], I will serve thee seven years for Rachel . . . and they seemed unto him but a few days, for the love he had to her." Proverbs 5:18, 19 exhorts: "Rejoice with the wife of thy youth . . . and be thou ravished always with her love"; and again, "Better is a dinner of herbs where love is, than a stalled ox and hatred therewith" (Prov. 15:17). Solomon's Song (8:6, 7) exhorts that marital love is to be set "as a seal upon thine heart, as a seal upon thine arm; for love is strong as death. . . . Many waters cannot quench love, neither can the floods drown it: if a man would give all the substance of his house for love, it would utterly be condemned."

University of Florida Sociologist Felix Bernardo, who is also editor of *The Journal of Marriage and Family,* reveals that from a survey of 1600 professional papers it's now virtually proven that premarital promiscuity, as much as extramarital philandering, is absolutely devastating to the institution of marriage, family and parenthood. It was a wonderful thing to hear Billy Graham and Pat Boone on TV with Dick Cavett, telling the world that the happiest marriage in the world is the one of a husband and wife to the exclusion of all others, entering into a lifelong relationship of love and fidelity to each other. *Scholastic Magazine* out of New York tells us that 86% of our teens aspire to this kind of marriage and parenthood in our homes. *The Literary Gazette* in Moscow reveals that Russian men currently "crave for a return to marriages and homes that are based on love, trust, tenderness, and women who don't booze, smoke, cuss and fornicate." I was looking at a paragraph from the Canadian Bill of Rights recently. It reads: The "Canadian nation is founded upon the principles that acknowledge the supremacy of God, the dignity and worth of the human person and the position of the family in a society of free men and free institutions."

"As for me and my house, we will serve the Lord" (Joshua 24:15) is as contemporary today as 4,000 years ago. The closest we ever get to heaven here on earth is in the Christ-centered marriage and home. It's costly: $64,000 per child for the average middle-income home: but it's worth it, because Christ paved the way. He paid the price. St. Paul wrote to the Ephesians: "Christ loved the church, and gave himself for it," so "husbands love your wives, even as Christ also loved the church, and gave himself for it. . . . Let everyone of you in particular so love his wife even as himself, and the wife see that she reverence her husband. Children obey your parents in the Lord: for this is right. . . . And ye fathers, provoke not your children to wrath; but bring them up in the nurture and admonition of the Lord . . . not with eyeservice, as men pleasers; but as the servants of Christ, doing the will of God from the heart" (Eph. 5:25, 33; 6:1, 4, 6). There's no marriage counselor, psychiatrist, or Ann Landers in the world who has as good advice as that for a happy home. And it works in Newfoundland or New York, in Salsbury or Seven Persons, Alberta. As the sun is the center of the solar system so the Son of God needs to be the Center of your home.

I was reading the Dear Abby column the other day. An individual who signed himself as "A Changed Man" wrote that he had made an awful mess of his life. But at 31 he had come around. He said: "I have taken Jesus Christ as my personal Savior and am truly sorry for my past mistakes. All I want is a second chance." And Dear Abby commended him.

Jesus Christ had compassion, not only for individuals and families, but also for crowds. "I have compassion on the multitude" (Matt. 15:2) He announced. The change of direction in modern political history is often traced to the French Revolution which allegedly was triggered by the haughty remark of Queen Marie-Antoinette. As she rode in her royal carriage in regal splendor that swirled around her through the streets of Paris, and was told that starving masses could not afford bread, she snapped arrogantly: "Let them eat cake!" When she was executed on the guillotine in October, 1793, she had few sympathizers.

Jesus, in contrast, was born into poverty, lived with the disenchanted, ate with sinners, and was always very much one of the people, even though He was sinless. Paul Harvey was asked if Jesus ever walked in the slums. "Yes," he replied: Jesus Christ walked in the slums more than any reformer in history. But loving its people as He did, He would take the slums out of people before taking the people out of the slums. H. G. Wells, fifty years ago, wrote, "I see humanity . . . scattered over the world, dispersed, conflicting, unawakened . . . all these people reflect and are part of the waste and discontent of my life." This was noble writing from an ivory tower in Oxford. But Jesus Christ was not a mere analyst or psychoanalyst. "Jesus was never off His cross," Joseph Parker once exclaimed. "If I were God, this world of sin and suffering would break my heart!" Goethe, the German, reckoned. Mr. Goethe, that's precisely what it did when Jesus hung on the center cross! There His great heart was broken that He might heal the wounds of a riven world. A headline features the fact that we

North Americans spend 3 billion dollars annually on soap—to wash our exteriors. Jesus promises to cleanse our interiors by His priceless shed blood. And it's a cure that works.

People today are into the herd thing like the little animals of the jungle who run together when the mighty lion roars. People are much like a banana: they fear that to leave the bunch would be to get skinned. They'd sooner be seen in a coffin than be out of the 'in' crowd. Where it's at, for them, is where the Joneses are. So they go gung-ho into some new faddist therapy, because that's where the cat is jumping. Today it leads into encounter sessions, sensitivity seminars, self-realization clubs, spiritualist séances, group sex or booze. Anything to thump the fear of being alone! Ann Landers is shocked, for example, with the fact that in the last few years the drunkenness margin between men and women has narrowed down from 20-1 to 2-1. A survey of New York women shows that when a woman divorces, she's twice as likely to become a drunk. Alcohol, then, is a weapon to combat the fear of being alone.

North American Indian Chief Bruce Starlight said publicly to Prince Charles in Calgary, "Alcohol, the biggest single killer of native peoples, is devouring us like the smallpox that annihilated whole nations of the North American Indian." Red Letter headlines now tell us that 12% of North Americans over 54 have a critical drinking problem due to fear of the loss of health, loneliness and the fear of death. I read a few months ago in *The Winnipeg Free Press* that liquor offences in Manitoba in some areas had trebled in the late seventies over the early seventies. In the whole of Canada alcoholism has rocketed up almost 100% in the last dozen years. One of Ontario's leading legislators warns, "Alcoholism is the number one problem facing our society." Our Federal Minister of Health, Marc Lahonde, has insisted that beer is more dangerous to our people than arsenic.

We need controls on the advertising of liquor. Throughout North America liquor is mentioned—on the average—every 10 minutes on the 30 most popular TV comedy and drama programs. Sociologist Dr. Warren Breed points up the fact that in the programs themselves, 52% of the drinking is done by the stars or heroes and only 10% by the bad guys. I read *McLeans* magazine. But I abhor the fact that there are 54 ads for alcoholic beverages in a recent 84-page edition. Just how twisted can we get our sense of values? I'm glad that someone like "the Fonz" told the American Congress and the young throughout North America that he does not drink and urged his fans not to. He said he respects his body too much to abdicate control of it to liquor. The Bible says that a Christian's body is the temple of the Holy Spirit, not a garbage can, a slop bucket, or the chief input into the sewer system, as the millions who lush it on booze imply. You don't need booze to be happy. Proverbs 28:14 declares: "Happy is the man that feareth always."

Fear in society is something for which Jesus showed great concern. Especially with the jamming of people into our cities today people are often terrified rather than befriended by the Joneses. A Hollywood film is entitled: *City of Sin*, a depiction of the kind of evil, crime and violence that dominate our metropolises in the West. A Futures Conference of people from the world is called to consider: "Cities, As If People Mattered." Jesus wept over the sins of Jerusalem. Why? Because its people mattered.

Moderns, especially in our cities, are intimidated by fear. The Gallup Poll now tells us that people on the whole value freedom from fear as their second most treasured human right. Yet, as Sir Hon. Harold I. Ickes has said, "Fear is in the saddle today." Everywhere we look, we seem to see Frankensteins. We're afraid of nuclear destruction. Premier psychologist Eric Fromm fears that with man beleaguered by the threat of war, overpopulation, "it is as if way down deep we have already concluded that catastrophe is inevitable." Then there's crime. Mike Maryn, a New Jerseyite, has been mugged eighty-three times. It is currently estimated that private security forces now far outnumber policemen. And there are as many private guards in uniform as there are members of the armed forces.

London's Joy Melville published a new book, *Phobias and Obsessions,* in which she states categorically that fears are sharply on the increase worldwide. Jesus prophesied this when He foresaw in the last days: "Men's hearts failing them for fear, and for looking after those things which are coming on the earth" (Luke 21:26). Melville points up 241 phobias that are currently attacking people, stating broadly that they fall into three categories: fear of a specific object, such as cats or spiders; fear of a specific situation, such as crowded places, a restaurant or an airplane; and fear of a specific illness—or of death itself.

Fear is a monster in society today. Steve Shutt, the Montreal Canadien superstar, laments, "I worry all the time about the future. You look at guys who were great in their day and then bombed out because of booze or women or they couldn't handle their money." Then there's Doug Jarvis, another star of the Montreal Canadiens. I was addressing several thousand young people at Praise '77 at Brantford, Ontario. When I came down off the platform, my niece Lynda introduced me to Doug. Smiling, relaxed, he seemed to be in a state of complete peace. Do you know why?

Because Doug, as a boy, gave his life to Jesus. Now Christ—not merely hockey—is his reason for living! He knows some of the glorious "fear nots" in the Scriptures. Our Lord said: "Fear not, little flock," "fear not, Abraham," "fear not, Jacob," "fear not, Moses," "fear not, Samuel," "fear not, Mephibosheth," "fear not, Daniel," "fear not, Mary," "fear not, Zecharias," "fear not, ye shepherds," "fear not, Simon," "fear not, Jairus," "fear not, Daughters of Zion," "fear not, Paul." Isaiah exhorted: "Fear thou not; for I AM with thee. Be not dismayed: For I AM thy God. I will strengthen thee; yea, I will help thee; yea, I will uphold thee with the right hand of my righteousness" (Isa. 41:10).

Perfect love casteth out fear" (1 John), wrote St. John. And that love is realized when we give our hearts to Christ, through whom we win over fear.

Finally, Christ has compassion for the dying. Jeremiah's Lamentations were written in a dying time for Israel, and constitute the most tearful book in the Bible. Yet it is right in the middle of this small book that we read: "It is of the Lord's mercies that we are not consumed, because his compassions fail not" (Lam. 3:22). When Jesus was in Gethsemane, He affirmed reassurance from His Father regarding His own death: "Who in the days of his flesh when he had offered up prayers and supplications with strong crying and tears unto him that was able to save him from death, and was heard in that he feared" (Heb. 5:7). This put Him into a position to resolve forever the dilemmas and dismays of His followers over the matter of death. Again, we turn to Hebrews (2:14, 15) and read that "as the children are partakers of flesh and blood, he also himself likewise took part of the same; that through death he might destroy him that had the power of death, that is, the devil. And deliver them who through fear of death were all their lifetime subject to bondage."

Death for the Christian, of course, is a triumph. St. Paul wrote to the Corinthians that for the Christian "death is swallowed up in victory. O death, where is thy sting? O grave, where is thy victory? The sting of death is sin; and the strength of sin is the law. But thanks be to God, which giveth us the victory through our Lord Jesus Christ" (1 Cor. 15:54-57).

For the Christless person, death is an ultimate and irreversible disaster! Nicholas Von Hoffman, the *Washington Post* columnist, points out that whereas the Victorians of a hundred years ago did their best to suppress sex in all its various manifestations, they revelled in death. Today the precise opposite is the case: it is in vogue for people to revel in sex while suppressing any overt references to death. Von Hoffman goes on: "There are probably millions of us who have seen other people mate but have never seen another human die. This is an absolute reversal of the Victorian death scene with the children and grandchildren and the great-grandchildren around the bed with the minister and friends of the family in attendance." Von Hoffman alludes to the emergent idea of their being "motels" for the dying, where they'll be removed from the concourse of other people. Dr. Ernest Howse writes on "The Hospice," as a hospital wing—or even a building for the dying. The grim prospect of death is getting to be too much for Christless moderns to handle.

Dr. Gerald Bristow, director of the University of Manitoba's Health Sciences Center, complained that terminally ill patients "are, by and large, lonely and unsupported at a time when support and honesty are most needed.... Patients ... fear death.... Physicians and nurses, by and large and for various reasons—perhaps the admission of failure or an expression of their fear to face their own mortality—shun individuals as they approach death." Dr. Bristow lamented the near total insensitivity for the pathetic "spiritual needs of dying persons."

Burt Reynolds, in his lead role in *The End*—a current film hit on dying, was being interviewed. He told Rex Reed that he's not merely afraid to die—he's terrified! "Howard Hughes couldn't buy his way out of death. Ari Onassis couldn't stop it. I will die, too, someday. But when the time comes, I think I know how I'll react—I will be a coward. I'll immediately try to make a bargain with God. I'll offer Him anything!"

Eddie Villery, Jack Benny's closest confidant, said after Benny's decease: "Jack had a terrible fear of death." To save himself from impending death, Bing Crosby assured that to delay the advent of the grim reaper: "I'd even sit in a volcanic crater in Hawaii if I felt it would do any good." When Hubert Humphrey was told he had terminal cancer, he called it "the worst moment of my life." Queen Elizabeth I, of England, for the last twenty years of her life wouldn't look into a mirror. She stubbornly wanted to envisage herself forever young. Billionaire Howard Hughes $2,000-a-day eight-room penthouse on the 20th floor of the Princess Hotel, Acapulco, Mexico, contained a laboratory equipped with oxygen tanks, electrocardiograph, centrifuge, medicine and other medical equipment. In spite of all this, he failed to live past his allotted three score and ten.

Dr. Elizabeth Kubler-Ross, the veteran Swiss Psychiatrist, has pioneered the "Life after Death" idea in modern medical circles, affirming that she no longer merely thinks there is life after death. She *knows* there's life after death. In her *Death and Dying* best seller and in her essay, *Death, the Final Stage of Growth*, she communicates convincingly her ideas to the world. Dr. Raymond Moody's *Life After Life* and *Reflections on Life After Life* are follow-throughs of Kubler-Ross' pioneering of modern man's need to face up to the reality of dying.

As death is the deepest nadir that a Christless person can sink to as a mortal, it is the highest apogee to which a believer in Christ can aspire—unless that experience is superseded by the second coming of Christ. The detached sophisticates of 200 years ago used to say of the early Methodists, for whom they otherwise had only derision: "They do die well!"

On Easter Sunday in 1977, I was preaching in East Toronto. In the evening service, several came forward to give their lives to Christ. After the benediction, Nan, a matronly, middle-aged woman, stepped up and asked me if I had held a crusade in Carrig Fergus in Ireland in the winter of 1955. Yes, I had. She said: "My brother, Bill, gave his life to Christ in that crusade, and also my sister, Sheila. Sheila was 32, a young mother. The month after that crusade, she suddenly died and went to heaven. A third sister was Jean. She, too, had two children. But she was not converted. Instead, after a period of unalleviated depression, she stuck her head in a gas oven on her 38th birthday and killed herself. Nan had thought about those two sisters for twenty years. She had emigrated here to Canada. For a long time she had wavered in the valley of decision—on the verge of verdict. But now, thank God, she had given her life to Christ.

6

Super Seer

In the film, Superman has X-ray eyes that can see through virtually anything. He knows everything about anybody with whom he has to do. This, of course, points us straight to Jesus Christ. When Jesus appeared to Peter after His resurrection asking: "Lovest thou me?" Peter replied: "Lord, thou knowest all things" (John 21:17). In John 1:24, 25 we read that "he [Jesus] knew all men, and needed not that any should testify of man: for he knew what was in man."

One of the world's greatest surgeons, Dr. Richard Selzer, publishes *Mortal Lessons: Essays on the Art of Surgery* in which he reckons that one of his biggest problems is that his public expects him to play God—to be "priests" and "saviors" as well as surgeons, to see through people and know everything that's wrong with them, and then to heal them. It's simply asking too much. That's why doctors have to pay as much as $30,000 per year in insurance premiums today, whereas only a few years ago $3,000 would be a top figure: because the public are desperate to find a Savior who knows all that's wrong with them and can guarantee to cure them of any illness.

Jesus, because He was God, had total analytical

powers to see into the human heart and diagnose what was wrong with people. There were times when He saw the best in them. But He also saw the worst. One day He described what "defileth the man. For from within, out of the heart of men proceed evil thoughts, adulteries, fornications, murders, thefts, convetousness, wickedness, deceit, lasciviousness, an evil eye, blasphemy, pride, foolishness: all these evil things come from within, and defile the man" (Mark 7:20-23). Right from the beginning of human history, our Lord was looking into man's heart with total perception.

A new best seller is *Desires of the Heart*. As those words in Shakespeare's *The Little Prince* state, "It is only with the heart one can see rightly." Dr. Christian Barnard implanted, with temporary success, the heart of a chimpanzee into a dying 68-year-old man. What man really needs "for keeps" is a "new heart" implanted from his maker, not a monkey.

There's no use adding spokes to the wheel when the hub is gone. The human race has hub- or heart trouble. "Dear Abby" observes from her mail that today's kids may be "getting smarter in the head, but at heart" they are deeply disturbed. You see, it's really from the heart that we do our living.

The wife of the President of Harvard, Dr. Bok, publishes a book in 1978, *Lying*, in which she reckons the average American tells 200 lies per day. There have been movies now on jaws, hair, eyes, voices, and fingers. God has a movie on "Heart." He knows and has on record, ready for the judgment day, what has gone on in all hearts since Adam appeared in the Garden.

And we're waxing worse and worse—lost, as it were, in a vast moral wilderness. Actress Margot Kidder complains of today's film plots: "The roles are all so nebulously written. There is no right and no wrong—simply different viewpoints. Heroes are easily confused with villains and even supermen and princes turn out to have feet of common flesh." The aging sage, Jean Good, when asked about the future of our society, replied: "Changes in the human heart, not more constitutional changes are needed to solve the problems" that we today face.

The New York blackout had some interesting lessons. U.N. Ambassador, Andrew Young, said that the darkness within the people was much worse than the mere darkness without. In Geneva at the time, Young went on: "Sin began with Adam. All men sin and fall short of the glory of God. If you turn the lights out, folk will steal. They'll do that in Switzerland too." A little boy fell from a dock into about twenty feet of water. Fortunately, a fisherman was close at hand, and he pulled the little guy out. "How did you come to fall in?" he asked. "I didn't come to fall in," the small person replied. "I came to fish." So man has fallen, in his blindness, into the pit of sin. Only Jesus can lift us out. There's a pop song: "I got lost in the dark—and then I found you!" Man gets lost in the darkness of sin, and his only hope is to respond to the Light—Jesus! In the words of Arthur Koestler's best seller, the human race is caught in *Darkness At Noon*—darkness in his heart at the very noon of his scientific flowering.

So what does the human race need? According to the Bible, we all need spiritual heart washing. Back on the farm in Saskatchewan during the depression, when I was a child, we had washday once a week, and it was a colossal undertaking. Dylan Thomas, in a black mood in *Under Milkwood*, lamented: "Nothing grows in our garden; only washing and babies." Well, back on our farm washday meant a big washboard.

And we'd take turns scrubbing out the overalls that were caked with farm dirt and grease. Then came a manually operated washing machine, manufactured with a rocker that brought blisters to the hands and aches to the small of the back. Then it was Maytag. Thank God for Maytag's gasoline motored washing machines. The gas hose would occasionally leak deadening fumes, and too big a load would slop soap bubbles over onto the linoleum. But it beat those corrugated washboards by a country mile.

Today people still can't make it without washday. The doctor is concerned with washing disease out of his patients' bodies. Housework is mostly washing, cleaning, scrubbing, rubbing.

Everybody knows deep inside that we all need to be washed within. In 1977 in India, the Kumbh Mela Festival, held every 12 years, assembled what's called "the largest gathering in the world"—ten million bathers in one day—to the Ganges at Allahabad to wash and hope to achieve "the purification of the soul and release from the cycle of death and rebirth which is their lot until salvation." Top of the pops in the seventies has been an old Gospel song: "Oh happy day, when Jesus washed my sins away."

In Isaiah 1 we read, "Wash you, make you clean. . . . Come now and let us reason together, saith the Lord. Though your sins be as scarlet, they shall be as white as snow, though they be red like crimson, they shall be as wool" (Isa. 1:16, 18). In a supermarket I saw advertised: "Bleach for the unbleachable." Well, that's a contradiction of terms, but it's expressive. Christ's blood was shed to cleanse from *all* sin. Certainly, to be washed spiritually we have to repent of our wrongs. Elton John sings "*Sorry* seems to be the hardest word." But that's what we have to say to Jesus. Erich Segal, in his runaway best seller, *Love*

Story, stated, "Love is never having to say you're sorry." To Christ, love *is* saying, "I'm sorry: sorry for my sins, Jesus!" As our Agape Team was driving out of Calgary we saw a collapsed bridge. Someone had painted on to it in huge whitewashed letters: "Dear Jesus, Please Help!" Yes, Jesus is always near to help—not to whitewash our exterior, but our interiors, to whitewash our sins away. The thing is, we have to respond.

I was preaching in Toronto recently and Andy Farino of Riverside United Church came forward to talk to me. A decade ago I held a crusade in the hockey arena in Islington. Andy and his wife, Margaret, and their children, Heather and Ron, attended. On a Friday night they had come forward and committed their lives to Christ, and He changed their hearts. Never since had they felt a desire to do other than to love and serve the Lord with all their heart, soul, mind and strength.

Six times in the Gospels we read that Jesus knew their thoughts (e.g., Matt 9:4; 12:25; Luke 5:22; 6:8; 9:47; 11:17). And when He had risen from the dead, overtaking the unsuspecting Emmaeus disciples, He knew the inmost thoughts that possessed them (Luke 24:38). In Hebrews 4:12, we are told He is the "discerner of the thoughts and intents"—that is, the pre-thoughts of a person. Indeed, in Psalm 139:2 "thou understandest my thought afar off."

Does He usually find good thoughts whirling around in man's minds? Regrettably, no.

St. Paul wrote to the Romans: "The carnal mind is enmity against God: for it is not subject to the law of God, neither indeed can be" (Rom. 8:7). To the Corinthians, St. Paul wrote of nonconverted people, however religious they may be: "Their minds [are] blinded [by a] veil untaken away" (2 Cor. 3:14). The next chapter tells us: "The god of this world hath blinded the minds of them that believe not" (2 Cor. 4:4). In Ephesians 4:18 we read of mankind "having their understanding darkened, being alienated from the life of God through the ignorance that is in them, because of the blindness of their heart."

Lord Elton, the Oxford don, insists that 83% of the content of the modern novel is based on perversion: crime, illicit sex, etc. Harold Robbins, who specializes in sex and crime novels, boasts that he has sold 90 million copies of his books. He points to the fact that eleven million Americans buy men's magazines every month, and with three reading each, that adds up to 33 million. That's one in every three American men poring over pornographic magazines every month. According to Legislator Arthur Lee, the average child spends 1,277 hours a year in front of a television screen (255 of these hours being commercials). In fact, by the time a senior graduates from high school he or she has been in school 11,000 hours, while, on the average, watching 18,000 hours of television and witnessing 18,000 killings. According to the *Dallas Morning News* there is 50% more rape committed by heavy TV viewers than by those whose TV viewing is limited. It was reported in mid-1978 that children may see their favorite primetime TV characters in as many as 40 intimate acts and drink alcohol up to 50 times a week, according to a Michigan State University study. The study, paid for by the U.S. Office of Child Development, is part of a study to determine what impact, if any, televised sex and liquor have on young children. The survey of 4th, 6th and 8th grade pupils found that their favorite shows were on at night. Few favorites were aired on Saturdays when there are children's shows. Between 7 p.m. and 9 p.m. in a typical week, there are 2.7 instances an hour of intimate sexual behavior between adults, and alcohol is seen on the tube almost 3.5 times an hour, as many as four times during crime shows. Most surprising was a finding that children see or hear seven times more references to sexual intercourse between unmarried adults than between husbands and wives.

Widely publicized in 1977 was the court case of Ronald Zamora, 15, of South Florida, who killed the woman next door exactly as he had seen it done on a Kojak episode. Zamora's defense lawyer claimed the lad had watched TV six hours a day for most of his life and when he had committed the crime he was "under the influence of prolonged, intense, involuntary, subliminal television intoxication" (*Time*). He was "electronically brain washed, living in a television fantasy world. The tube became his parents, his school and his church." Is it really any wonder that there is such a wide mental acumen gap between the older adults of our times, who never have watched much television, and the new generation of youth?

There was a time not long ago when it was thought that education and the Kingdom of God were nearly identical. That's completely exploded today. The Hall-Dennis Report of the sixties is as out of style as the Pyramids . . . dispelled chiefly when, for a time, it seemed that the conduct of university residents more resembled a penitentiary than a Jesuit seminary. So today we see such headlines as: "Cheating Now a Part of the University Scene" over an astonishing article by McMaster's Professor James Daly. *The Winnipeg Free Press* runs a headline; "Now Mindless Intellectuals." James Vold writes of the tragedy of attempting "ethics, not prayers, in our classrooms." He explains that we are fast discovering that true prayers and genuine ethics are inseparable. Francis Schaeffer says that if there is no absolute by which society is to be judged, then society is absolute. And where does this intellectual posture of secular humanism lead? The full vicious circle goes back to what Thomas Hobbes said about life: It's "solitary, poor, nasty, brutish and short."

There is a whole new attitude today about Christ, the Bible and the Holy Spirit being God's final Word of authority to man. James Reston (*The New York Times*' successor to the late Walter Lippman) wrote recently about how refreshing it is to have a man like Jimmy Carter as President, chiefly because of his belief in the authority of the Word of God and the absoluteness of truth. The Dead Sea Scrolls and now the 15,000 Elba tablets in Northern Syria have been strongly confirmational of the Bible. So impressed was *Time* with the findings in these Elba tablets relating to Biblical history that it asserted, "Fundamentalists should have a field day with this one."

Miki Bratt (also in *Time*) states, "The burning question that we all are trying to answer is: Is the human species doomed to destroy itself?" The answer is: yes, unless man turns to God. God reveals himself in His Word. I think that John Lennon was speaking for millions of new generation youth when he said that though he had no time for the church, he has been reading the Bible and he digs it. Keep digging, John! Fifteen million more North Americans put their trust in the truth of the Bible than in the truth-telling capacity of the media. Catholics are reading the Bible today and have set aside a week each November as National Bible Week. And so are the Jewish people. Both communities are reading it as their masses haven't for a thousand years. Prime Minister Begin of Israel is the first of that country's Prime Ministers to be a total believer in the absolute truth and trustworthiness of the Old Testament. Here is why the Bible is far and away the world's best seller! Bible distribution reached the incredible total of 331 million worldwide last year: nine percent above the previous year.

It is refreshing that the secular press has recently been challenging the honesty of the so called "best-seller lists." Although *The New York Times Book Review*'s best-seller lists are now compiled from computerized sales figures from more than a thousand bookstores, they remain incomplete. So do those of *Publishers Weekly*. The reason: neither includes sales from specialized religious bookstores.

According to *New Times*, which offers "The Real Best-Seller List" in a recent issue, *The New York Times* simply regards religious bookstores as "a separate breed." For example, *The New York Times* list did not include *"How to Be Born Again"* by Billy Graham, in 1977, although it had sold 650,000 copies of its first printing of 800,000; and a second printing of 250,000 was on order. By comparison: Woodward and Bernstein's *The Final Days* was said to have topped the *Publishers* Weekly best-seller list with a total of only 630,000. But the real best seller was Kenneth Taylor's easy-to-read translation, "The Living Bible." Sales were 2.2 million. Notes *The New Times*: "To be sure, most of the people we know who follow best-seller lists are not interested in how the works of Kenneth Taylor and Billy Graham are doing." But omitting them from the so-called best-seller lists obliges one to turn to a compilation like *The New Times* to find out what books people are really buying. What is really fascinating is that Japan's best-selling book in 1977 was the Bible, even though the population is overwhelmingly Buddhist. There were 1,480,000 copies sold in bookstores, with total distribution (free and paid) through all channels topping 10 million. With a 1% Christian population, Japan was the only country in the world where the number of Bibles sold in a year exceeded the number of Christians.

An interesting article appeared in *Time* stating that "when the American Bible Society issued its homespun *Good News Bible* translation, some critics responded. *The Philadelphia Inquirer* stated that *Good News* is bad news, in terms of poetry, of grace, of charm and thus of beauty.' Many readers apparently disagree. In three months the new version has sold 1.5 million copies at $2.50."

To ignore the Word of God and take the Christless route can only end in disaster. An intellectual who went that way was Dylan Thomas. According to *Time* it was in 1953 during his final trip to the U.S. that Thomas conducted his famous bender through New York's Greenwich Village. Delirious with drink and looking like a decayed cherub, he collapsed in his hotel room. He died four days later of what one physician termed "a severe insult to the brain." In dramatic contrast, on national television on the Hour of Power, I heard a new Christian, a black Californian, declare that since Christ came into his life, instead of injecting dope into his veins, he's injecting hope into his brains by daily poring over the Word of God. The look on his face could be described as spiritual intoxication.

Charles Dickens observed: "The Bible is the best book ever known or ever will be," while one totally committed to its message, David Livingstone, wrote: "All that I am I owe to Jesus Christ, revealed to me through His Divine Book." The foremost male skier Canada has ever produced is Jungle Jim Hunter, who puts down his powers of concentration to his meditation on the Scriptures during times of high stress. Certainly reflection on the Word of God is better mental therapy than Gestalt, TM, Transactional Analysis or psychotherapy. One of the sickest societies in the world is Hollywood. Yet there are so many psychiatrists' clinics around there that one square is nicknamed "the mental block." St. Paul wrote to the Corinthians that our minds through commitment to the Word of God can be built up by "casting down imaginations, and every high thing that exalteth itself against the knowledge of God, and bringing into captivity every thought to the obedience of Christ" (2 Cor. 10:5).

When Billy Graham was in Toronto for a Crusade in 1955, Nelles Silverthorne was one of Canada's very distinguished surgeons, as he still is today. He had been a close friend of the givers to the world of insulin, Banting and Best. He himself was the one who gave to the world vaccine for whooping cough. He was also a founder of the world famous Hospital for Sick Children. But he didn't have "the indwelling Christ," as he puts it. A surgeon friend took him out to hear Billy Graham. His own account goes: "On my way home from one of the [Billy Graham] meetings, I pulled my car to the curb and I confessed my sins and with great sincerity asked the Lord Jesus to come into my life and change me. I knew that Christ had died for me and shed His blood for my sins, and I felt hopeless about giving up some of my sins. . . . Soon it became apparent that this internal desire or power—His Holy Spirit—came into my life, a true supernatural power . . . and revealed the truth of 2 Cor. 5:17: 'Therefore if any man be in Christ he is a new creature.'" For 23 years, Dr. Nelles Silverthorne has been one of Canada's most dynamic lay witnesses for Christ. And with his razor-honed mind, he has written: "The Relevance of Biblical Truth to the Practice of Medicine."

Then again Jesus Christ has eyes to see through

our bodies. "The body," wrote St. Paul to the Corinthians, is "for the Lord, and the Lord for the body" (1 Cor. 6:13); and to the Philippians he aspired that "Christ might be magnified in my body" (Phil. 1:20), for Christ "is the Saviour of the body" (Eph. 5:23).

So Jesus Christ is very much aware of all that goes on in our bodies and therefore very concerned about the conduct of our bodies. St. Paul testified to the Corinthians, "I keep under my body, and bring it into subjection: Lest that by any means, when I have preached to others, I myself should be a castaway" (1 Cor. 9:27). Here he was addressing himself primarily to sexual sin. We're living in an age when most feel that because we've got the pill to prevent pregnancies, antibiotics to knock out V.D., legalized abortion for those who happened to be careless, and loosening mores that the matter of sexual discipline should be largely abandoned.

But it isn't working out that way. According to the Canadian Planned Parenthood Association report of mid-1978, "three-quarters of sexually experienced girls are not using contraceptives. Fifteen percent of girls become pregnant the first time they have intercourse with a boy." How is this affecting the statistics? Currently, "the number of single teenagers having babies is rising by thirty percent a year."

So what happens? Japan has one abortion to every two births, and North America is not far behind. In Canada we've had "325,000 'therapeutic' abortions"—as everyone knows, most of them expediently rationalized by the slightest whim. Abortion in North America is going up as much as 20% per year: at a time when test-tube babies, babies from artificial insemination, and cloning have become a near obsession with many.

And the very V.D. we thought could be eliminated

by antibiotics is today pandemic. Reports in 1978 are that gonorrhea has become North America's number one reported communicable disease, more than three times as prevalent as the number two disease, chicken pox, with syphilis coming in an ugly third.

And with sexual discipline being abandoned, we're now told that ten percent of the population is homosexual. Currently one woman in a hundred is a prostitute. In Toronto the Good, two metro-women reporters in May, 1978, took careful count and claim they were propositioned a total of 100 times in an hour by aggressive, leering, obscene gesturing, horn-blowing, car-door opening, whistling, exhibitioning, verbally inviting men—of all ages. Is there no decency or guilt left? The former seems minimal. The latter is devastating. A recent study revealed that three-quarters of the men who die while in the act of intercourse, do so while having relations with a woman who is not their wife.

As if this is not enough, there is a new crusade on by the libertines to legalize incest. In her new book, *Incest: Sex Within the Family*, Helen Colton, Sc.D., reckons: "Left to our biological drives and desires, we human beings are capable of and desirous of warm, close, sensual and sexual expression with our blood kin." One thing is sure. If the church loses its vigilance, the legislators aren't going to hold the fort, according to what has been happening in high political circles the last few years. New York Psychiatrists Dr. Sam Janus and Dr. Barbara Bess publish their book *A Sexual Profile of Men in Power* in which they divulge how low some of our highest legislators will go to try and gratify their voluptuous passions for kinky sex, often sacrificing their reputations, integrity, health, wealth—and, the Bible adds, their immortal souls—on their immoral depravities. From Toronto the Good,

Canada's largest city has turned its historic downtown Yonge Street into a sinstrip of 42 sex shops, rivalling the worst of the degenerated gutters of any North American Inner City. A 12-year-old shoeshine boy is enticed by four wicked, vicious men—very sophisticated people to their friends—into Charlie's Angels Rub Parlor, which advertised: "Come to the world of love. Your happiness may depend on it." For Emmanuel Jacques, it meant apparently a vicious sexual rape by four lust-hammered homosexuals, and then cold blooded murder through a cruel, forced drowning in a sink. That's how sordidly sin sinks its victims. It advertises love and rebounds in hate. Heralded happiness meant heartbreak in an outpost of hell. Sin is forceful all right! Psychologist Dr. Paul Cameron calculates from polling people that one in four would murder if the price were right and they thought they could get away with it.

The answer to our bodily needs, as we've pointed out, is Christ. In April, 1977, I was conducting a crusade in a beautiful auditorium in Riverside, California, with 50 or 60 churches. One night I met the most fascinating man, the Rev. Philip-Blade-Smith. But instead of being draped in clerical garb, he was in motorcycle togs—obviously a biker. With him were his chopper colleagues: Pig Pen, Meatman, Black Jesus, Deacon, Vulture and Big Daddy. They were ex-roisterers with the motorcycle gangs: the Hell's Angels, the Coffin Cheaters, The Misfits, The Hangmen, The Highwaymen, The Devil's Own and the Chosen Few. Now they were all-out Christians riding for the Lord with Philip Blade-Smith's national organization "Christ's Patrol." "Christ's Patrol" had 500 bike gangs for Jesus—if you will—in 40 cities. I had seen them at mass Jesus rallies around the Continent. They earn their own bread, then ride their bikes for the Lord. Much of their witness is assisting people—especially other bikers—on the roads. They then either endeavor to give their testimony direct and lead those whom they've helped to Christ, or at least hand them a card which reads: "You have just been assisted by Christ's Patrol, M.C. . . . Christ is your Answer."

Philip-Blade-Smith was brought up a tough kid. Beat up early, he took a job in Dayton, Ohio, lifting 120-pound iron mouldings and built himself a muscular physique. He was a rebel without a cause. Then one day, having boozed too much, he was on a terrible downer. His workmate told him about Christ. He fired back that if ever the Name of Jesus Christ was thrown at him again, except in curses, he'd put out the guy's lights. You know what happened. A few days later he was led to the Lord and all out for Jesus, and founded "Christ's Patrol." Today, all across the Continent you can find these leather-jacketed bikers, only now instead of being chain-swingers and acid-droppers looking for a rumble, they fly a red and gold cross and crown. They're filled with the Holy Spirit out there in the highways and hedges, compelling the lost to come to Christ's house.

It's a great consolation that Jesus has eyes to see through our spirits. He can see the "poor in spirit" (Matt. 5:3); those "of a sorrowful spirit" (1 Sam. 1:15); those of a "perverse spirit" (Isa. 19:14); those who've lamented, "I had no rest in my spirit" (2 Cor. 2:13); or "I was grieved in my spirit" (Dan. 7:15); or those who feel "my spirit was overwhelmed in me" (Ps. 142:3); or those who opine "in the anguish of my spirit" (Job 7:11).

John Denver topped the world's record sales last year. But, he says his spirit hits record "lows." "I get so depressed sometimes . . . I ache inside, my heart broken, my spirit empty." Sometimes, he says, he gets obsessed with "suicide" hankerings. In 1978 Countess Margrit Piatti, the Swiss glamour queen, living in a luxury-studded penthouse "beautiful, rich, brilliant," blew out her brains with a hand gun. Her spirit was completely broken. In upper New England, where the traditionally self-contained Yankees live, suicide is almost double the national average. *The Cincinnati Post* quotes Psychiatrist Dr. John J. Schwab as lamenting that it's the young today whose spirits are breaking: "Depression and suicide among American youth have become massive health and social problems that are reaching epidemic proportions." He quotes the case of a girl, 16, who before killing herself wrote: "Dear Mom and Dad: I've thought it over carefully and I've decided life is just too much of a hassle. Please don't blame yourselves. You've tried really hard and I know you love me and I love you. I just want all the feelings to stop. P.S. I fed Buffy and changed her litter box. Please take good care of her for me."

Ann Landers highlights a letter from a 16-year-old girl (which unleashed a torrent of letters). It goes: "I'm sick of this house, sick of this town, sick of being under my parents' thumb, sick of being treated like a baby. Sick of being lonely even though I have lots of friends, sick of this lump in my throat, sick of almost running away but losing courage at the last minute, sick of the authorities who don't know the wonders of pot but keep screaming about how harmful it is. Sick of not being able to cry. Sick of needing to be somebody and knowing I never will. Sick of wanting revenge against people who have hurt me. Sick of wondering if I am really insane."

The Chicago Tribune carries an article on child suicide, a phenomena which is blowing like a blizzard across the peoples of the West. Example: "A 10-year-old, supposedly ignored by his family, put a noose around his neck, stood on a chair, and asked his brother to pull away the chair. The brother refused, so the 10-year-old kicked it away and strangled." His spirit was broken earlier than most.

Of course, over all, older men continue to lead the suicide parade.

How do we stop it? Certainly psychiatry or medicine can't stem the tide. In 1978, a shocking increase in suicides among British medical doctors has been registered. One in fifty male physicians ends his own life. In the U.S. psychiatrists commit suicide at seven times the national average!

In 1978, over half of high schoolers have tried to lift their spirits with pot. Nineteen percent of Americans between 18 and 25 have tried cocaine. But throughout most of the world alcohol is the primary means of trying to heal breaking spirits. Solomon gave us the Proverb (17:22): "A broken spirit drieth the bones." In the U.S. and Canada one in ten in the Armed Forces is a drunk. In two decades the number of women, compared to men who are alcoholics has risen from a 20-1 to a 2-1 ratio overall. The Betty Fords and Joan Kennedys are typical of what is now commonplace. Dr. William Ghent, addressing the Canadian Medical Association Council, states unequivocally that "the fastest growing disease in Canada today is alcoholism." The latest from the Soviets is that alcoholism in Russia is 74% higher than in the U.S. or France.

St. Paul gave us the solution to alcoholism: "Be not drunk with wine, wherein is excess, but be filled with the spirit" (Eph. 5:18). The key is His spirit filling our spirits, without which we are chronically and hopelessly empty. In Psalm 51 we read that God is waiting to fulfill the "broken spirit."

On the day of Pentecost, when they were all filled with the Holy Spirit, Peter rejoiced: "Thou hast made . . . me full of joy" (Acts 2:28), and in Acts 13:52 we read that "the disciples were filled with joy, and with the Holy Ghost." This experience, of course, is provided by Jesus Christ, of whom John the Baptist announced: "He shall baptize you with the Holy Ghost and with fire" (Matt. 3:11). Jim Elliot, martyred twenty years ago by the Auca Indians, prayed: "Oh God, keep me from asbestos Christianity. Make me ignitable." Clare Booth Luce was recently asked: "What do you think of Jimmy Carter?" To which she replied: "I applaud him for recognizing the two great needs of our country: physical energy, such as oil, and spiritual energy." The Holy Spirit is the Great Energizer.

Two or three years ago, we held a meeting in the Detroit area, and Dean, a boy of 11, came forward. Blind, his mother left him when he was 6. His grandmother brought him to our meeting. Coming forward to give his life to Christ he prayed: "Thank you for coming into my heart, Jesus, and thank you that I won't be lonely any more." He was filled with the Holy Spirit and the glory of the Lord.

Finally, Jesus Christ has the eyes to see into our wills. Emmanuel Kant insisted there's nothing good without the good will. Jesus is terribly concerned about our wills. To those around Him who refused to believe, He lamented: "Ye would not come" (Matt. 23:7).

Perhaps the greatest saint since St. Paul was St. Augustine. But he stumbled for years in the valley of decision imploring: "Give me chastity and continency, but do not give it yet." The late Werner Von Braun was asked: "What will it take to get man to the moon?" "The will to go!" was his curt but sure reply.

What will it take for you to go to heaven? Saying "I will!" to Jesus. Oh, that the 4 billions on earth would choose Christ in this very timeless moment. This is man's moment of truth. The Rolling Stones have a song: "This Could Be the Last Time." For every lost soul throughout eternity there'll be the recollection of "the last time"—when opportunity ceased to knock. For those who do come, in the words of a book title, "The Door Is Always Open."

I received a letter from Detroit recently from my friend Al Kuhnle, on whose radio program I had spoken. A high school girl had written in: "Thank you for telling me about Jesus Christ, for if you hadn't, the next week I wouldn't have been here!" She was confused, depressed and had walked out to the center of the Ambassador Bridge which joins Canada and the United States and climbed into position to jump. For her it was the bridge between heaven and hell. She was about to jump for hell. Then the voice of Jesus spoke through His Word. She called in for help and was converted. Today she belongs to a Christian growth group.

7

Super Sonic

One of the remarkable things about Superman is his capacity to be anywhere in nearly no time. Even after a hard day's work, he could travel faster than a speeding bullet. On one occasion he flew right around the world in ninety seconds flat. That's a million miles an hour.

Jesus Christ, as God the Son, came in from outer space at inestimable speed. And in His ascension He went to His Father at incalculable speed. Then He came back to meet Saul of Tarsus on the Damascus Road and John the aged on the Isle of Patmos. In John 20:19 we read that "at evening, being the first day of the week, when the doors were shut where the disciples were assembled for fear of the Jews, came Jesus and stood in the midst." (26) "And after eight days again . . . came Jesus, the doors being shut, and stood in the midst." And He can still say today to anyone who will listen: "Behold, I stand at the door, and knock: if any man hear my voice, and open the door, I will come in to him, and will sup with him, and he with me" (Rev. 3:20).

The Psalmist David expressed how the Lord was everywhere, all the time. "O Lord . . . thou hast beset me behind and before, and laid thine hand upon me.

Such knowledge is too wonderful for me; it is high, I cannot attain unto it. Whither shall I go from thy spirit? or whither shall I flee from thy presence? If I ascend up into heaven, thou art there: if I make my bed in hell, behold, thou art there. If I take the wings of the morning, and dwell in the uttermost parts of the sea; even there shall thy hand lead me, and thy right hand shall hold me. If I say, surely the darkness shall cover me; even the night shall be light about me. Yea, the darkness hideth not from thee; but the night shineth as the day: the darkness and the light are both alike to thee. For thou hast possessed my reins" (Ps. 139:1, 5-13).

Jesus Christ is not only wonderful, because He can do anything, and because He knows everything, but because He's everywhere. David simply could not, even if he had wanted to, "flee from" the Lord's "presence."

You see, Jesus Christ is present where there is need.

Luke the physician noted that when the people were besieged with needs, Jesus would appear. And whenever He did "the power of the Lord was present to heal them" (Luke 5:17) precisely as He had been more than a thousand years before, when the Psalmist wrote, "The Lord is my refuge and strength, a very present help in trouble." One of the most beautiful illustrations of this is recorded in John 4:46-56 where we read of a nobleman whose son was sick in Capernaum. So he took a day long journey to Galilee where Jesus was and besought our Lord to come and heal his son, who was on the verge of death. So Jesus healed him, not by remote control, but "by being there." He was everywhere. So the nobleman began his journey home and was met by a servant who told him that his son had been completely healed at precisely the hour Jesus said it.

So Jesus is the very present help in time of need. Surgeon D. Forrest Cioppa of the Kaiser Hospital in Walnut, California, has devised a scheme whereby he records on tapes soothing messages for patients before and after operations. He has thirty-one suggestions which, as the patients play, they hear whispered into their ears. They are to picture in their minds their favorite place of peace and tranquillity and to stay there mentally until they awaken. When it's over, they're told that all is well. The operation was a success.

Dr. Cioppa, in a study of 42 patients, calculates that 17% of the tape listeners left the hospital sooner than the non-listeners. And the tape listeners also required 36% fewer pills for pain or relaxation.

All of this, of course, is substituting a surrogate for the real Savior. Jesus says that He'll always be with us to relax and rest us, provide for us, protect and bless us. When Moses felt he was completely alone, in his advocacy of the Lord's cause to Israel, he went before Jehovah in prayer, imploring: "Now therefore, I pray thee, if I have found grace in thy sight, show me now thy way." And the Lord replied: "My presence shall go with thee, and I will give thee rest."

Today all kinds of exploiters prey on the restlessness of Western society. Psychologists Erich Fromm, Carl Rogers, Abraham Maslow, Rollo May and a myriad of others are putting forward their formulas, and millions devour their works as if they were gods of therapy. Dr. Wayne Dyer has his best seller, *Your Erroneous Zones*, in which he advances prescriptions for eliminating guilt, worry, blame and depression. In contrast, Judith Golden engenders guilt, worry, blame and depression by going before the American Psychiatric Association to make a plea for "self-pleasuring." She insists that men and women don't need each other to alleviate their sexual compulsions. Indeed, no one needs anybody.

History marches on, but it doesn't change very much. Modern medicine has nearly emptied our T.B. sanitoriums, but an underground tunnel has run a much larger percentage through to psychiatric hospitals. "What am I eating wrong?" a woman with ulcers asked her doctor. "Ma'am, it's not what you're eating, but what's eating you! And I have no cure for that." Jesus does. He said: "I do cures today" (Luke). At mid-century the North American men who had ulcers outnumbered the women 20-1. Now it's 2-1 (the same statistics as alcoholism). Psychiatrist Mary MacEwan is staggered by the number of top executives who are folding up. We've tried to organize a society from the womb to the tomb; from the sperm to the worm; from the time of people's hatching through their matching to their despatching. But man gets more agonization than organization. Women in unprecedented numbers who try to be the most chic, chicken out to manic depression. Now that they've crusaded and won their rights, Dr. Myra Weissman of Yale and fellow psychiatrist Dr. Gerald Klerman of Harvard insist that women overall are succumbing to double the depression manias that men experience. Freddie Printz, at 22, drives a bullet through his head. His manager is at one side; his psychiatrist, at the other. His mother and estranged wife are on and off the phone, while 40 million people are waiting to see him in "Chico and the Man." But no! As he wrote in his suicide note: "I can't take it any longer." Tommy Bolin, "Deep Purple" guitarist, does the same. I was at Oxford University in England with Kris Kristofferson. He's got smarts as well as smiles. But, bugged with life, he's been a heavy boozer. "It's the 'despair,' the terrible 'despair,' of my life," says Kris.

People today, according to Harvard's Professor Harvey Cox, are desperate for fulfillment. Their "money does not lust after houses, cars and clothes, but travel, drugs unusual sights and sounds, exotic tastes, therapies, and new emotional states." Peerless Hockey Goalie and brilliant Lawyer, Ken Dryden, the Montreal Canadien, lamented, going into the playoffs: "This is the time of the year when you wish someone else would possess your body." Mr. Dryden, Jesus Christ will possess your body—and your soul. Coming "to me," assured Jesus, "ye shall find rest unto your souls" (Matt. 11:29).

Secondly, Jesus Christ, is not only where there's need but also where there's faith.

He assured His followers: "If you have faith as a grain of mustard seed, ye shall say unto this mountain, Remove hence to yonder place; and it shall remove; and nothing shall be impossible unto you" (Matt. 17:20). What grieved Jesus most about His disciples was their lack of faith. Calming the storm on the Sea of Galilee, He remonstrated: "Why are ye so fearful? how is it that ye have no faith?" (Mark 4:40). Many times He sighed: "O ye of little faith" (e.g., Matt. 6:30; 8:26; 14:31; 16:8). And when He saw belief in the most unlikely people, He exulted that He'd not seen "so great faith, no, not in Israel" (Matt. 8:10) or, "O woman, great is thy faith" (Matt. 15:28). Pronouncements like "Thy faith hath saved thee" (e.g., Luke 7:50) and "Thy faith hath made thee whole" (e.g., Mark 5:34; 10:52) He used constantly when someone was miraculously recovered by His healing hand. Faith is at least as large a factor in the Epistles as it is in the Gospels. Hebrews 11 focuses exclusively on faith. In verse one we read that "faith is the substance of things hoped for, the evidence of things not seen"; and in verse six, "Without faith it is impossible to please him; for he that cometh to God must believe that he is, and that he is a rewarder of them that diligently seek him." So crucial is faith in Jesus' assessment of human response that Jesus asked: "When the Son of Man cometh, shall he find faith on the earth?"

Gilbert K. Chesterton, thought by some to be the foremost philosopher of his time, reckoned that all you needed to know about a man to understand him was what he believes. An example was Nietzsche, the philosophical father of Naziism. Nietzsche claimed his religion was a "transvaluation of values." He declared: "A new commandment I give unto you. Become hard. For the best things belong to us . . . and if men do not give them to us, we take them."

It's not only amazing what the masses do believe: it's astonishing what they *don't* believe. After the moon walk, pollsters revealed that an incredible one-quarter of the American public didn't believe it had actually happened. The testimony of Neil Armstrong made no indentation on their unbelief. After all, with a technology as advanced as that of the United States they were sure it would be no trouble at all to perpetrate a hoax on any scale imaginable.

One of the encouraging happenings of our time, of course, is the number of people who are being born again. According to the Gallup Poll, there are 50% more born-again Americans than it takes to elect an American president. Christ is present where there is faith. But, better still, He changes those who have faith!

Jesus Christ is the real "Leader for a Change" (President Jimmy Carter's campaign slogan). Liv Ullman entitles her best seller: *Changing*. Jesus Christ is the real changer. *The National Enquirer* recently commented that Elizabeth Taylor simply "can't change her way of life." Greta Garbo, now into her 70's, recently broke a 30-year self-imposed silence about her personal feelings to say, "I have made a mess of my life and it is too late to change it." The Bible says that "in Christ" it's never too late to be "changed . . . by the Spirit of the Lord."

If we'll change our minds, God will change our hearts—and our lives. Of course, as Thomas Carlyle, premier philosopher of his day, wrote, "Change indeed is painful yet ever needed." Well, the most pain anyone ever encountered to change you was Jesus' awful pain on the Cross. "Change," wrote Richard Hooker 300 years ago, "is not made without inconvenience." It's notable that we change clothes—often several times a day. We change addresses, on the average, every two years. We also change partners. Currently there are as many divorces being issued as marriage certificates. Some people change their names. The three Gabor sisters have had eighteen names. I have friends who change their phone numbers and the locks on their doors every few weeks. People change their hairdos, their glasses, their features, and their figures. They change jobs. They change friends.

TV commercials tell us to change cars, trucks, tractors, breakfast foods, soaps, beverages. We're now told that 86% of sporting events on TV are sponsored by breweries and distilleries, trying to get viewers to change their drinking habits. *Change* is actually the *name* of a tobacco brand.

Recently we received a letter: "I am 14 years old and have committed myself to Jesus. Since I've been saved, my life has changed completely. I have spoken to people I used not to like, and have smiled at them when before I couldn't stand even to look at them. It seems that if I ask God for things I need, He gives me an answer and usually gives me what I ask for. Everything has changed." Actually the only really meaningful change is the one Christ effects when we put our faith in Him as Savior and Lord. And once we're Christ's, He's our great enabler. A good word to the new Christian is that slogan of Coach Roger Nielson of the Toronto Maple Leafs: "Success comes in cans—not can'ts." With faith in Christ, St. Paul reckoned, "I can do all things through Christ which strengtheneth me" (Phil. 4:13).

Thirdly, Christ is present—in a special and unique way—where His Church is gathered together.

Jesus promised His presence: "Where two or three are gathered together in my name, there am I in the midst of them" (Matt. 18:20). In Hebrews 10:25 we are admonished: "Not forsaking the assembling of yourselves together, as the manner of some is; but exhorting one another: and so much the more, as ye see the day approaching." The ancient Psalmist (84:1, 3, 4) exulted: "How amiable are thy tabernacles, O Lord of Hosts! My soul longeth, yea, even fainteth, for the courts of the Lord; my heart and my flesh crieth out for the living God . . . . blessed are they that dwell in thy house: they will be still praising thee!" David had a throne on which he sat as a king. In the Lord's tabernacle of those days, they sat on the floor. David preferred to sit on the floor in the Lord's house to sitting, crowned, on a throne in his palace.

Today, the deadest place an unbeliever can be is the house of God. For the true believer in Christ, the liveliest and most meaningful place on earth to be is in the church. The Harvard trained author of several best sellers, John Updike, observes tartly that "in general the churches . . . bore for me the same relation to God that billboards did to Coca-Cola; they promoted thirst without quenching it." Jesus Christ "loved the church and gave himself for it" (Eph. 5:25). And if He loved the church, it's imperative that we understand what the church is. In fact, eternity depends on it.

In virtually all of the 100 countries in which I've travelled people are saying, "But isn't belonging to a church being saved?" Not necessarily. William Brown Bowdle went to Sunday School—and church—every Sunday for 99 years. But as he himself insisted, going to church didn't make him a member of the true church of Jesus Christ. No one, church member or not, is a bona-fide member of the true church of Jesus Christ unless he's been saved.

Today "born again" is the most familiar description of what it means to be a Christian. It is a phrase that is on nearly everyone's lips. Jesus said: "Ye must be born again!" (John 3:7), and that's why we "must be born again." But the phrase "born again" is used only 4 times in the entire Bible. The word "conversion" is used in one or another of its forms about 15 times in the Bible. Let's not forget that Jesus insisted, "Except ye be converted . . . ye shall not enter into the kingdom of heaven" (Matt. 18:3). So unless you're converted, there's no way you can go to heaven. That's what Jesus said. But the word "saved," in one or another of its forms, is used 350 times in the Bible. It is by far the most often used word to describe those who are rightly related to God through Christ.

St. Peter declared unequivocally and without qualification or apology: "Neither is there salvation in any other: for there is none other name under heaven given among men whereby we must be saved" (Acts 4:12). He did not suggest the possibility of merely taking the matter under advisement.

Jesus tells us in John 10:9: "I am the door: by me if

any man enter in, he shall be saved, and shall go in and out, and find pasture." Saved! That word conjures up a lot of impressions in our minds. A hockey goalie makes about thirty saves per game. A baseball relief pitcher might manage twenty or so saves in a season. A crop is saved by a good rain. A surgeon saves a patient's life by the educated skill of his hand on the scalpel. A policeman saves a child from drowning. Churchill saved England from Hitler. Erica Jong writes her best seller, *How to Save Your Own Life*, which, with the way it defies morality and deifies immorality, might better be entitled *How to Ruin Your Own Life*. Whole pages in magazines and papers are sold to bank advertisements which invite your: "SAVINGS—That's What It's All About." "SAVE NOW—During our Annual Sale" publicizes every store worth its salt, sooner or later. A headliner during the Rumanian earthquake disaster reads: "Buried for 62 Hours, Waitress Saved in Bucharest." Yet when the word is used spiritually, it is nearly unknown. The Dean of our Billy Graham Center at Wheaton, Illinois, ran a survey in the Chicago area of what people thought was meant when asked if they were saved. Replied one: "What I wished I'd have done with my last paycheck." Another thought it had something to do with acquiring "Green Stamps or something."

About 65 years ago an English lad, on a visit to a rural community in Scotland, set out to enjoy a swim in a small lake. Seized with a cramp while some distance from the shore, he shouted for help. A young farm boy plunged into the lake and brought him to the shore. Years passed before the two met again. The city youth asked the boy who had saved his life what plans he had for the future, and learned that his ambition was to study medicine. So the youth's parents, who were wealthy, gave the young farm lad the money needed for his education. He graduated and embarked on a career of scientific research. In 1928 he found a new drug called penicillin and became famous as Doctor Alexander Fleming.

The London youth also had risen to fame. He went to the Near East to meet Roosevelt and Stalin during the Second World War, and was there stricken with pneumonia. His condition was critical, so penicillin was flown to him and his life was again saved. For the second time, Alexander Fleming had saved the life of Winston Churchill, then Prime Minister of Britain. Spiritually speaking, Jesus Christ made possible your salvation not by discovering a wonder drug, but by giving His life for you on the Cross.

I was in a crusade in Texas. The opening Sunday night I felt an urgent compunction to preach on "We must be saved!" Many came forward that night to put their faith in Christ as Lord. The next Sunday evening, after preaching, I was talking to a lineup of people. One was Dr. Kenneth Bockhorn. He was bubbling. A nominal Lutheran all his life, he had been depending on the merits of his churchmanship for salvation. But his life had been coming apart at the seams! Then Doctor Bockhorn came to the Crusade, realized that he had never really been saved, and came forward truly to "believe to the saving of [his] soul" (Heb. 10:39). Now he was in the same Church as Martin Luther, who after being a churchman and priest for years, was only truly born again into the universal Church of Jesus Christ when he was "justified by faith alone."

Fourthly, Jesus promised to be specially present with us when we engage in world evangelism.

Before He ascended He promised His disciples, who went unto all the world to preach the Gospel,

"Lo, I am with you alway, even unto the end of the world" (Matt. 28:20).

To Paul, Jesus appeared. Why? We read in his testimony to Agrippa: "I have appeared unto thee for this purpose, to make thee a minister and a witness," giving him a personal undertaking to be constantly delivered "from the people, and from the Gentiles, unto whom now I send thee" (Acts 26:16, 17). Dr. Robert Speer of Princeton said a half century ago: "No one is really walking with Christ who is not willing to walk with Him to the ends of the earth." James Gilmour used to say that he once adhered to Jesus' saying in Mark 16:15: "Go ye into" Mongolia. Then he read from Acts 16:9 and realized that Christ's Word was also: "Come over into" Mongolia. One looks at the imbalance today. While two-thirds of the world waits in spiritual darkness, never having once heard the Word of the Gospel, during the years 1973-77 (according to the United Kingdom Missions Handbook), the number of foreign missionaries shrank by 25%.

Meanwhile, what about our homelands? In the U.S., in 1978, there is a substantial oversupply of clergy in the Presbyterian, Methodist, and Episcopal churches, to name only three. In fact, the Hartford Seminary Foundation reckons that the Episcopal Church is "already so over-supplied that if current trends continue, there will be an Episcopal priest for every lay member of that denomination by the year 2004."

The answer, of course, is to evangelize! It was heartening to hear early in 1978 that President Carter "plans to become a foreign missionary" after he leaves the White House. "I would like to be a part of being able to turn that country back to God. I hope someday that's what I'll get to do." Roger Nielsen, perhaps one of professional sports' most dedicated coaches, reckons that his highest aspiration after he leaves the bench is to "become a missionary . . . . I think that's more important than coaching a hockey team." Immediately be became Pope, John Paul I declared that the primary task of the church is to evangelize. The late Pope Paul, in the last year of his life graphically observed that our commission from Christ is more the "bread and wine" than "the bread and the fishes." The world's spiritual hunger is even greater than its social needs.

World evangelism is, of course, an all-out undertaking. World missions statesman, Oswald J. Smith, insists that the key is: "Be a man without sidelines." Lady Astor was asked if she thought Anthony Eden would make a successful Prime Minister. "No," was her reply, "he doesn't have the fire in his belly." It takes the inner fire to evangelize. Winston Churchill once observed: "We may all be worms, but I aspire to be a glow worm." Christians are people who should glow with the love of Christ. H. Belight Nelson reckons: "When I put on God's apron He sent me into the kitchen." Billy Sunday was once in a church which was dead and he got up and said: "This church is so cold that the ushers should be wearing ice skates to take up the offering." The late Paul Little observed that it was not that the Gospel had lost its power. It was that the church had lost its audience because it had lost its shine.

I was preaching in Florida while a bike race was on, and the announcer's voice penetrated my hotel room. He exclaimed that a French Canadian had shot into the lead, his apt description being: "He's going as if he's fresh out of hell!" On Hockey Night in Canada, Andy Bathgate was asked for the toughest superstar he ever had to play against. "Bobby Hull! Because he played every game as though it were to be his last." Every time a Christian witnesses, he ought to be like that. As Vance Havner puts it: "There are many church members who are talking about going out on the limb to bear fruit, who have never climbed the tree."

The principle of evangelism is that each one is to reach one. Preach—knock off the "P" says "reach"; knock off the "r" says "each." So preach means reach each. An old Indian proverb says: "Give a man a fish and you feed him for a day: teach a man to fish and you feed him for a lifetime." Jesus told us to be fishers of men, not tenders of the aquarium. The reason Jehovah's Witnesses have doubled their numbers in the seventies is because they're out there witnessing, while many churches are holding bazaars and banquets and finance seminars on how to keep the store. And the Jehovah's Witnesses don't find it easy. According to *Time*, for each of the 196,656 people baptized last year the Witnesses conducted 740 visits to people's homes and distributed 1,650 copies of their various books and magazines. In June, 1978, we were all announcing that the 43,000 who gathered in Toronto to hear Billy Graham was the largest religious gathering in the history of Canada. The very next month, the Jehovah's Witnesses packed 75,000 into the Olympic Stadium in Montreal. It's a truism that twenty-seven million North Americans have been corralled by the new cults, because too many evangelicals are no longer out there in the market place—on the frontier—in the store fronts and on the street corners. Jack Hiles claims to have the largest Sunday school in the world because he's got people with "Baptist heads, Pentecostal hearts and Jehovah's Witness feet."

We need to take a page or two out of the communists' book. Just this year, according to BBC, "the Soviet Union has replaced the United States as the world's most prolific overseas broadcaster." Sergei Mechayev's Revolutionary Catechism reads: "The revolutionary is a dedicated man. He has no personal inclinations, no business affairs, no property, and no name. Everything in his life is subordinated towards a single exclusive attachment, a single thought, and a single passion—the revolution . . . . He has torn himself away from the bonds which tie him to the social order and to the cultivated world with all its laws, moralities and customs. . . . The revolutionary despises public opinion. . . . Morality is everything which contributes to the triumph of the revolution. Immoral and criminal is everything that stands in his way. . . . Night and day he must have but one thought, one aim—merciless destruction. . . . He must be ready to destroy himself and destroy with his own hands everyone who stands in his way."

When the Archbishop of Canterbury spoke at Wycliffe Theological Seminary in Toronto in celebration of its hundredth anniversary, he reckoned, in his plea for a fresh proclamation of the evangelical gospel, that African Christians could do a great deal to evangelize us in Canada and Britain. Asia has suffered heavy persecution. In Cambodia alone, since it went Communist, a million and a half of the total population of seven million have been liquidated. Many of these were Christians. There are terrific pressures and imprisonments imposed on dedicated Christians in Communist countries. But they've never asked us for sympathy—only our prayers and love. There's more happening spiritually behind the Iron and Bamboo Curtains today than ever before. Soviet law prohibits the propagation of religion, but the saying has never been truer that the blood of the martyrs is the seed of the church. There are many moving accounts of Christian women regularly visiting graveyards where they find bereaved people willing to talk about the hope of eternal life in Jesus Christ. Also, Soviet Christians often turn their weddings and funerals into evangelistic meetings. Millions of Christians today are "within," or, as we say today, "underground." But it's an underground railway—to heaven!

I received a letter in mid-1977 from a twenty-year-old lady. I won't disclose her name nor her location. It reads: "My husband is threatening to kill me for receiving Christ. He has brandished his axe in anger several times! He swears that he will follow me wherever I go and kill me along with our children. Please help me!" Some treat Christianity as a picnic, while these are in panic. Some of us need to get deeper, much deeper, into the river of God's will. Many of our prayers misfire right on the launching pad because we begin with our thoughts rather than God's thoughts. God's plans always involve a process which moves in a period of time—God's time. So we've got, in the words of recently converted pop star Scot Wesley Brown, to learn to walk our talk. That's what a disciplined disciple is: someone both walking with, and talking for, Christ! You see, the secret of answered prayer is to find out what God is doing, and to do the same thing.

Finally, Christ will be present with believers when He appears to receive them home at His coming again.

We read that "to them that look for him shall he appear the second time without sin unto salvation" (Heb. 9:28).

The body of Charlie Chaplin was stolen, so there's apparently been an "anti-theft tomb" built for him in Switzerland. Neither situation will be a problem to God when the time comes for Chaplin's resurrection. Jesus said that eventually all who are in the graves will come forth. Earl Hughes, who died in 1958, weighed 1,069 pounds. It occurred to me that if he believed on Christ, even that poundage would not keep him down when Christ comes again. God has some very strong and persistent angels. I saw a headline the other day which stated that "Angel Dust Is the Newest Drug Fad" to get kids high. That I don't know much about. But I do know that the Bible says that angels will get saints the highest they've ever been, up from the dust of this hopeless world to be on high with Christ forever—without ever having that trip terminated. It's been announced that the engine to propel Enterprize into space in 1979 is costing one billion dollars. Friends, the price Jesus paid to get us up into outer space was His pricelessly precious blood. Lucille Ball laments that in today's world "it's sad for the young people because they have nothing to look forward to.... The new generation is already sullied by hopelessness." The Bible tells us that Christians are those who are "looking for that blessed hope and the glorious appearing of our Great God and Saviour Jesus Christ" (Titus).

"The Eagles" pop group drew Canada's largest concert crowd of 1978, and the huge headlines featured: "Eagles Fly Into Outer Space." It may be asked, "Why do people crave for an experience of rising from the earth to the heavens?" The TM'ers are now outrageously claiming to do so. The answer is that the human psyche longs to rise from this earth into the skies, to escape from planet earth. The other day 24-year-old Californian Brian Allen, the bicycle racer, won $85,000 from the London Royal Aeronautical Society for self-propelling himself off the ground and through the air in a 70-pound plane with a 97-foot wing span over a 1.4-mile figure 8 park. He was the first in history to lift himself that far through the air.

Others have been caught up into the air: like Enoch and Elijah in the Old Testament, and Philip and Paul in the New.

Olivia Newton-John sings, "I'll fly away." It's up to her whether she actually will or not. What I do know is that the Bible assures us in words made memorable by Cardinal Cushing's recitation of them to a billion people watching on television at the time of John Kennedy's funeral: "The Lord himself shall descend from heaven with a cry of command, with the archangel's call, and with the sound of the trumpet of God. And the dead in Christ will rise first; then we who are left, shall be caught up together with them in the clouds to meet the Lord in the air; and so we shall always be with the Lord. Therefore comfort one another with these words" (1 Thess. 4:16-18, Douay Version). These, of course, were not just empty words. They were demonstrated in the ascension of our Lord. C. S. Lewis used to tell us often at Oxford about the coming again of Jesus Christ and our need to be ready. One of his most potent homilies was: "Aim at heaven and you will get earth thrown in. Aim at earth and you will get neither." Another is, "Sorrow looks back, worry looks around, faith looks up." That's where I'm looking: not to the crowd, but to the cloud; not to a trench in the cemetery, but for the trumpet in the sky: whence Christ shall come again. I saw a headline the other day: "10,000 Man-Made Objects in Space"—all put up there since Sputnik twenty years ago. I thought of Jude's prophecy: "Behold, the Lord cometh with 10,000 [not sputniks] angels." *Time* editor Frederic Golden publishes his new book on *Colonies In Space*, in which he projects what the Enterprize is aiming at—a settlement of human beings up in the sky. Most dramatic of the ton of wreaths at Elvis Presley's funeral was one shaped for the King of Rock 'n

Roll—like a crown on which sat a real telephone with the receiver dangling off the hook. The Christian is not listening for Elvis to talk back; but looking for Jesus to come back, to appear for His own.

Late in 1977, I was holding a crusade, using our multi-media visually to illustrate my points while speaking on that solemn passage from 2 Peter 3 where we are warned of the heavens passing away with a great noise, the elements melting with fervent heat, and the earth and its works being burned up with fire. Present was university physicist, Professor James Jones, his wife and family. All of them came forward to commit their lives to the risen Lord. Professor Jones, as a scientist, knew better than I did what St. Peter was predicting. And consequently with his family, he resolved that he wanted to be ready for Christ's coming again.

8

Super Supplier

Another analogy in Superman to the Christian faith is that he saves the lives of the imperilled and supplies their needs. In one of the most impressive scenes in the whole film, Superman sees a scruffy, terrified cat marooned on a limb fifty feet up, without hope of saving itself. Superman swoops down and sweeps it into his grasp. Then there is an incident in which the President's plane is about to crash in a terrible thunderstorm. In spectacular fashion, the Man of Steel defies the gale and rescues the Chief Executive. There are numerous cases of people receiving Superman's specialized attentions while in a variety of insoluble situations. He always arrives at the right time, and in the right manner, and supplies their needs.

Jesus Christ is involved in the minutest details of the lives of God's children. He once said, "Are not two sparrows sold for a farthing? And not one of them shall fall to the ground without your Father . . . The very hairs of your head are all numbered" (Matt. 10:29, 30).

When we think of Christ supplying the believer's needs (not his *greeds*), we must start with the soul. The part of man's make-up which refuses to be at peace until attended to is the soul. There are a great many descriptions of troubled souls in the pages of Scriptures, ranging from torn to bowed down to anguished and melted. And since the soul is the very essence of a human being, its care and repair are crucial. To neglect the soul led a man like Baron de Montesquieu to wail, "We should weep for men at their birth, not at their death." Headlines tell us, "Behind That Clowning There's A Bitter Red Skelton," underscoring the fact of one more soul not at rest. Ed Ward's syndicated Hollywood column observed, "There is a new royalty ruling today's record charts, led by artists such as Linda Ronstadt, Stevie Nicks, Carly Simon and Joni Mitchell. They are queens of Rock . . . who have conquered a macho industry . . . sex, money and highs of every kind are abundant." Ward insists that, in contrast to their extravagant life-styles, they are anything but fulfilled people. Their souls are strangely empty.

People of the seventies have tried hard to fulfill themselves. They have become what Tom Wolfe called the "me decade." It is a time in which everyone from best-selling authors to clergymen are advising us to reach for emotional freedom, and release our angers and frustrations in the soothing ambience provided by the therapeutic profession. The 1970's are an era, Robert Fulford reckons, when "holier-than-thou" has been replaced by "loonier-than-thou." Even mental instability has gained a certain status as a means of asserting a distinctive self-identity in an otherwise "blah" society. Today's people compare psychiatrists as their parents once compared preachers. Moderns embrace eccentricity and lapse into neurosis as an escape from fear. They go into psychosis as an escape from terror! In the box office hit *Network*, the hero goes crazy. But crazy is a poor replacement for Christ.

Gaining a better self-image through going to a shrink is a poor substitute for gaining salvation through Christ.

The American political scientist, Irving Kristol, in a *New York Times* piece distinguishes between the radicalized students of the sixties and seventies and those of the thirties. Radicalism today, he says, "seems to be more psychological than political. There is a desperate quest for self-identity, an evident and acute involvement of one's political beliefs with all kinds of personal anxieties and neuroses, a consequent cheerlessness and truculence."

Out of this emerges a new attention to the soul. Whoever, a quarter-century ago, would have believed that "soul albums" would one day be best-selling recordings! Most Americans thought that souls were something you might give a bit of attention to on Sunday morning. But today's society is crying out for soul salvation. *McCalls* surveyed 60,000 readers in mid-1978 and discovered that 80% believe that their soul is the real person in them—the part which lasts. Mohammed Ali said in Atlanta recently, "What matters is your soul." Late in life, Werner Von Braun avowed that ultimate reality could only be achieved by those who have an unwavering "belief in an immortal soul, a soul which survives death and goes on from judgment to eternity."

Prime Minister Trudeau was asked by *McLean's* what his ultimate aim was. He replied that he wanted to get away from the public into a place of "solitude and silence" where he could settle the matter of his soul needs.

O. J. Simpson has been one of the most idolized and eulogized athletes of recent years. Recently he complained that his soul wouldn't let him rest. "I sit in my house," he laments, "and sometimes I get so lonely it's unbelievable." O. J. admits, "Life has been good to me. I got a great wife, good kids, money, my own health—and I'm lonely and bored. I'm saying, 'Juice, life really can be something.' I often wondered why so many rich people commit suicide. Money sure isn't a cure-all. That's why I throw on my jeans and try to stay loose."

Psychiatrist means "physician of the soul." Some think that C. P. Snow, the Britisher, is currently the world's greatest mind. He is physicist, philosopher, chemist, etc. In his learned Klopstag Lecture in Chicago for 1977, he said bluntly: "Psychoanalysis doesn't work." On the other hand, the great Christian psychiatrist, Dr. Klaus Thomas, calculates that after twenty-five years, he's convinced that the answer to guilt and soul lostness is faith in Christ: "I have no doubt about the overwhelming harmonizing, health restoring, and transforming power of a genuine Christian faith."

The Bible declares: "Thy soul shall be required of thee" (Luke 12:20). So what are we to do about our souls? "Hear and your soul shall live," urged Isaiah (55:3). Peter exhorted, "Commit the keeping" of your "souls" to Christ, "as unto a faithful Creator" (1 Pet. 4:19). "Receive with meekness the engrafted Word, which is able to save your souls," admonished James (1:21). On that great day of Pentecost, we read that there were "added to them 3,000 souls" (Acts 2:41). "Believe to the salvation of the soul," we're instructed in Hebrews (10:39), the result being "an anchor of the soul, both sure and stedfast, and which entereth into that within the veil, whither the forerunner is for us entered, even Jesus" (Heb. 6:19, 20).

As *The New York Times* said, Dr. George Faust is only the most notorious and most representative of the millions in history who have "traded their immortal souls to Satan for wealth, power, knowledge, and pleasure." In contrast, Lady Ann Erskine was, two centuries ago, the most influential female Christian in Scotland. She became a great force for Christ when she was a beautiful young woman. It all began one day when she was out riding in her regal bedecked coach. She saw a large crowd assembled. She tapped her coachman on the shoulder and asked, "Who is that man addressing that huge gathering, there in the open air?" She was told that it was Rowland Hill, the great Welsh preacher.

"Drive over and let me hear what this curious fellow has to say!" she instructed. As she pulled up, Rowland Hill immediately recognized her. He stopped for a moment and turned boldly toward her. Fearlessly he declared, "I have something for sale! It is Lady Ann Erskine's soul! Who will bid? Yes, Satan! What is your offer? 'I will give riches, honor and pleasure!' shouts the devil.

"Jesus Christ speaks up: 'I will give eternal life!' " Lady Ann Erskine was angry. But superseding her indignation was the unmistakable call of Christ to her soul. She descended the gilded steps of her coach and knelt beside a gleaming wheel on the turf. She cried out, "I will have Jesus!" And Scotland has never been quite the same since.

Jesus Christ not only supplies our soul needs but also our personal needs. He makes us whole. When He was confronted with needy people, like the one who for thirty-eight years had been a paraplegic, He asked, "Wilt thou be made whole?" And when the man assented, Jesus commanded—regardless of his excuses—"Rise, take up thy bed and walk" (John 5:6, 8). He did and Jesus pronounced: "Thou art made whole" (v. 9).

This concept of wholeness was passed on to Jesus'

disciples and after our Lord's resurrection and ascension, we read that the apostles would step up to people who were crippled and impotent and say: "In the name of Jesus Christ of Nazareth, rise up and walk."

I'm convinced that Jesus Christ is still asking us: "Wilt thou be made whole?" Whole from your debilitating lust, your crippling fear, your debauching drunkenness, your manic depression, your violent temper, and the hold of tobacco. There are so many defeated people around today. In mid-1978, Barrie Wexler wrote an astonishing seller: *How to Survive a Modern Relationship: A Manual for Complete Losers.* Wexler stated in a promo interview, "There's no way to survive a modern relationship. None of the techniques described in my book ever worked for me."

A few years ago, everybody—and I mean just about everybody—was unloading on the medical profession. Now Ellen Goodman of Boston writes that until recently, "doctors explained very much and patients trusted very much. There was a time when doctors scribbled commandments on pads of paper, and patients followed them to the indecipherable letter. They spoke medicalese and we translated through ears blocked by fear. We gave up the care of our bodies to the doctors, the way we gave up the care of our souls to the clergy. Now, having been supplicants of doctor worship, we're becoming a nation of medical atheists. Having discovered that medical people are fallible, we've lost our faith altogether. It isn't just skepticism that's replaced our former belief; it's rampant distrust."

Doctors themselves are the first to tell us that they can prescribe aids to healing and remove obstructions to health, but that they have limitations. E. Stanley Jones used to tell of the skillful surgeon who was so much Christ's that he said: "I hardly know where my hand-work in an operation ends and His begins." As Oral Roberts is quoted in *Time*: "The healing streams of prayer and medicine must merge."

While I was writing this chapter, I came across a UPI story. "Ex-Fattie Neva Coyle" of New Brighton, Minnesota, tells her story: "Three in the afternoon, just before the kids came home from school and time for an afternoon 'fix' of crackers, cream cheese and jelly. When you've weighed as much as 248 pounds and fought a weight problem for 35 years, the afternoon snack becomes a daily battle. I thought there had to be a way to get the battle out of my mind," Mrs. Coyle said. "I whirled around and wrote on a piece of paper attached to the refrigerator, 'I give this up to you, Lord.' The battle for that day was gone. The next day I wrote it over again. Sometimes twice in one day. I wrote it down over and over and again and again. I didn't feel so helpless any more." Out of her successful fight against fat came the birth in April, 1977, of Overeaters Victorious, Inc. (OV). It is growing so fast the now-attractive mother of three has a difficult time keeping up with the administrative matters that go with it. She says, "OV is an association of born-again Christians who are exercising their faith in a real problem area of overeating and overweight." She is her own walking testimonial to the efficacy of faith. She now weighs 149 pounds with, as she said, "10 more pounds to go." "Like everyone else, I tried everything else first," Mrs. Coyle said. "I've been through all the major loss programs. In a moment of desperation, I had intestinal bypass surgery. I lost 60 pounds, but I gained it all back. I finally called on God to help. I've weighed 148 pounds for more than five months. It's the longest time I've been thin in my life. Food doesn't have priority any more." Overeaters Victorious stresses strong supportive action among members. Members also are required to read the writings of two living saints in the movement—Frances Hunter, author of *God's Answer to Fat*, and Joan Cavanaugh, author of *More of Jesus, Less of Me*. Mrs. Hunter warns that the thin, hard line to slenderness calls for disciples to "only buy foods that Jesus, John or Peter would buy." "If God made it," she wrote, "and man didn't change it, then you can eat it. God gives us the good stuff. I can't imagine Jesus Christ coming out of the supermarket with 12 bags of chips—one for each disciple." Mrs. Coyle knows the job is difficult. "The first step is a study of the Bible, which shows us that compulsiveness of any kind is a spiritual problem, not a physical one," she said. "There is something lacking in you spiritually. You have to put that calorie in your mouth before it turns to fat. We try to deal with people on how to keep that fat out of the mouth. It's hard, we realize, to learn to listen to God, learning how to draw on faith. It's there. It's in there. It's hard to get that faith out." And so emerges another Christ-inspired movement to see ailing people made whole.

There are millions striving for victory over cigarette smoking. While men are smoking very slightly less than they did a decade ago, women are smoking much more. According to William H. Foege, speaking before the U.S. Senate, in a six-year-period "there was an eightfold increase in the number of 12- to 14-year-old girls who smoke cigarettes."

There are other millions striving for victory over alcohol addiction. In Russia, in 1978, Soviet authorities are near desperate in their quest for a cure for alcoholism, where it is responsible for the "majority of suicides, accidental deaths and crimes" and divorces. In Canada, over the last quarter of a century deaths from cirrhosis of the liver (alcoholism) have jumped past lung cancer and suicide as a killer (all three are escalating). And we're told that consumption of alcoholic beverages will be doubling in North America by the early eighties.

There is victory in Christ! St. John wrote that: "Whatsoever is born of God overcometh the world: and this is the victory that overcometh the world; even our faith. Who is he that overcometh the world, but he that believeth that Jesus is the Son of God?" (1 John 5:4, 5).

U.S. Chief Justice Warren E. Burger says that three-fourths of all U.S. trial lawyers accept cases beyond their ability. One beautiful thing about being a Christian is that "we have an advocate with the Father, Jesus Christ the righteous" (1 John 2:1). We are well represented, being assured that the ascended Christ is certainly "able to save them to the uttermost that come unto God by him, seeing he ever liveth to make intercession for them" (Heb. 7:25).

It's so wonderful that Jesus Christ is personally concerned with our personal problems. "Appalled" writes to Dear Abby: "What is your opinion of a therapist who asks his patients to tell their troubles to a machine? Yes, it's true! I went to a psychologist who calls himself a 'doctor,' and he asked me if I had equipment at home to make and play back tape recordings because that's the latest thing in counseling. He says I should make a tape of what I want to say, and he will make a tape of his reactions, and we can both play them when we have time and are in the mood. Is he some kind of nut? Or are machines now replacing doctors?" I will not quote "Dear Abby's reply. I will say that it's really freaky, how many bypasses people will take to go around Jesus Christ.

Jesus Christ also supplies our needs as families.

I can think of no slogan more needed today than the one on the often-seen plaque, "Christ is the head of this home." The state of marriage and the family is in such chaos throughout the world as to merit profound universal concern. There are half as many divorces as there are marriages in the U.S. today. Marriage is too easy. There's a saying: "We're all becoming Californians." In California, "instant" "confidential" marriages are fully legal, and some authorities reckon that it's not just a matter of traditional bigamy flourishing. Many—a far higher percentage than most people think—have as many as ten "marriage" partners without ever having bothered to get a divorce. According to *The Los Angeles Times*, more today opt for "trial marriages" than oppose them. *The New York Times* says that many single women are deliberately having babies, just for the experience. Then there are pre and extramarital pacts being signed by couples entering into "marriages," which entitle them to engage in all kinds of unmarital conduct. The consequence is that in the last decade there has been a sevenfold increase in the registered number of couples who are living together without any serious intention of getting married.

People in breaking or broken marriage situations are running to "counselors"—just as they did back in Ezekiel's or Jeremiah's day—instead of to the Lord. Psychologist Dr. L. d'Addario, of the University of California, says that perhaps 30% of all female patients who consult professionals—such as psychiatrists and social workers—are "sexually approached by their counselors."

Thank God that from the secular world signals are more and more explicit that sexual promiscuity and permissiveness don't really work. A Gallup Poll reveals that nine out of ten young Americans aspire to permanent marriages rather than temporary affairs. In the early seventies, Nena and George O'Neill authored their immensely popular *Open Marriage* in which they pioneered the concept of spouses accepting extra-marital affairs. Now they've gone back on that fallacy, and in *The Marriage Premise*, Nena O'Neill leads with the revamped view that "sexual fidelity is not just a vow in marriage or a religious belief, but a need associated with our deepest emotions and our quest for emotional security."

Doris Hopper, in the *Toronto Star*, points to Bill Williams, 30, and his wife Marion, 30 (not their real names), a Metro professional couple. After eight years of faithful marriage and one child, both tried outside affairs. They found their marriage nearly went down the drain until they helped salvage it by making a re-commitment to each other.

"We decided to concentrate on each other. That cancels out having affairs. There just wasn't time for that," said Mrs. Williams. They said their marriage is one of the few to remain intact among a group of married friends who entered into the spirit of sexual experimentation that broke loose in the early seventies. "All of our friends are divorced and into their second marriages. We're just into our second round of our first marriage," said Mrs. Williams. The couple recently had a second child—"shortly after we made these new decisions." Having affairs with others meant the couple had "some heavy, heavy, painful times." She had had at least two outside affairs. So did he. "The other people in the outside relationships were starting to make demands, wanting commitment, and stuff like that," she said. "While feeling secure enough to let your mate play around sounded like a fine idea, it hurt," the couple found. "I think no matter how liberated you want to call yourself, you will feel jealousy and hurt. You can't transcend that stuff when your husband doesn't come home all night or when your wife stays away for a weekend," said Mrs. Williams. There was talk of splitting up. "We talked and decided our priority would be to be with each other. What that meant was being together, expressing our feelings to each other, being dependent on each other. There was no time for other relationships outside of marriage," she said.

There are other tragedies in addition to the grief infidelity in marriage inflicts on the partners. Researcher Roger Langley, co-author of *Wife Beating: The Silent Crisis*, tells us that in 1978, there are 31 million married women in North America being beaten up by their husbands and eleven million battered husbands. "Two million allegedly suffer severe beatings every year." According to the Ann Landers' column, 1.7 million American couples have gone after each other with guns and knives. As many as a third of the murders of married persons were performed by the victims' spouses. In the Boston City Hospital "about 70% of all assault victims cared for in the emergency rooms were spouses who had been attacked by a husband, a wife or a lover."

This not only alienates marrieds from each other; it does irreparable damage to the children. Fathers and mothers neglect their offspring in order to pursue their infidelities, or to try and heal the wounds of a battered marriage. So a current international survey shows that the caveman cartoon character, Fred Flintstone, is identifiable to 90% of American 3-year-olds, while 44% of 4-6-year-olds perferred "television to daddy."

What has happened is that there's a reaction to Dr. Benjamin Spock and Dr. Lee Salks' liberal notions about parenting—which simply didn't work. For example, Dr. Bertram Cohler, of the University of Chicago, in his intensive research for the U.S. Government concerning child-rearing, swings sharply to the right with his findings "that kids of the Great Depression in the thirties turned out to be better adults than the coddled kids of the sixties, raised by liberal parents in the child-be-all period." Cohler believes the miserable showing of youngsters in the sixties is proof that the liberal theories in the child-raising arena didn't work. "And that's why we're throwing out a lot of theories," concludes Cohler.

Certainly Cohler's concerns are justified by the sexual chaos into which teenagers have fallen in the mid and late seventies, often because they've had such indifferent parenting and neglected homes. Sociologists Melvin Zelnik and John F. Kantner, of John Hopkins University, in their *Family Planning Perspectives* (1978) shocked millions with their research conclusion that "a nationwide report on adolescent sex shows a one-third increase between 1971 to 1976 in both premarital sexual activity and pregnancy among girls 15 to 19 years old."

So who cares? Jesus Christ does! He came as the great reconciler of family relationships. He heals husband/wife ruptures and turns them into raptures. He repairs parent/child alienations and turns them into alliances of love. He set forth His principles through His apostle Paul: "Husbands, love your wives, even as Christ also loved the church, and gave himself for it," and "wives, submit yourselves unto your own husbands, as unto the Lord. For the husband is the head of the wife, even as Christ is the Head of the church." "Children, obey your parents in the Lord: for this is right," and "ye fathers, provoke not your children to wrath: but bring them up in the nurture and admonition of the Lord" (Eph. 5:25, 22, 23; 6:1, 4). As the sun is the center of the solar system to sustain, lighten, and heat it, so the Son of God is the sustainer, light and warmth for a Christian home.

In 1977 I was conducting a crusade in Colorado. One evening a deeply troubled woman came forward to commit her life to Christ. A deeply troubled man came from another part of the great college gymnasium. They each met Christ. Looking around, they saw each other. They were husband and wife—and separated. But now they were Christ's and became one again, went home together and began a brand new marriage.

Then of course there are the ten million widows in North America, the three million widowers and the million unattached divorced persons! What is their hope if they're Christians? That Christ is with them!

Then again, Christ supplies our material and vocational needs. Jesus never shirked His responsibilities as an ancient citizen of Israel and inhabitant of the Roman Empire. When He needed tax money, He sent His disciples to receive a coin from a fish's mouth to pay the tax. He did not fudge on their obligations to the civil government. He put the whole thing in perspective when He took a coin in hand and, holding it up to the crowd, urged people to render unto Caesar the things which are Caesar's, and to God the things which are God's.

Jesus believed in the work ethic. He supported the concept that we earn our bread by the sweat of our brow, and that by the application of the same principle we make our faith known. All of His chosen disciples were working people.

Work is a very relevant issue today. Christ obviously is very concerned about His children's employment. Martin Luther used to ask new acquaintances, whom he knew to be Christians: "I know that serving Christ is your vocation, but what's your occupation?" That was the right emphasis. William Wallace is so right to stress that "labor isn't secular, labor is sacred. After we've become Christians, God expects us to be the salt of the earth in the office, the classroom, the factory," and, of course, the farm.

But I doubt if Christ is really served, when the organized church keeps jumping into politics as a corporate lobbyist. It did so a hundred years ago, almost exclusively on the side of right-wingism. Today it's the social activists who are at it, always on the side of left-wingism, and in 1978 the WCC donates $75,000 to the guerrila groups in Africa to overthrow governments. To me, the work of the Church is not political revolution. It is the presentation of Christ. Pope John Paul II has made his view very plain that CHRIST himself in His Gospel is the Light of the world. No sophisticated socialist who's never had his hands dirtied, or his face grimy, should be allowed to steer the church, when he has nothing to offer but the mouthings of a left-leaning London School of Economics professor.

Such self-styled instructors take it upon themselves to teach some of the dedicated practical economists with the latest intellectual liberal intimidations, which occasionally have the workability of a mischievous chimpanzee with a blow torch in a dynamite factory. Equally destructive is the cantankerous redneck who shakes a Bible, as if he were Moses descending from the Mount, at all compassion-driven social reformers who genuinely yearn to lift up the fallen, feed the helpless hungry, house the squalid and educate the aspiring illiterate.

Nor is Christ best served by the multi-millionaire who travels between his air-conditioned home, and air-conditioned office in an air-conditioned car and then pays $50 to go over to the steam room at the club and sweat. I believe every North American Christian should welcome the current emphasis on simplifying our life-styles.

A Christian is a "workman, that needeth not to be ashamed," whose goal is to be "approved unto God" (2 Tim. 2:15). He's someone eager to roll up his sleeves for labor; not to roll into the sack when the sweat or tears begin to roll down his cheeks. A Christian is called to a battlefield, not a playground. He is someone who is always out there giving. For some, work is an occupational hazard; for others, to be out of work, a personal disaster. But we can be sure, as Ann Landers wrote to a hard-working lawyer's wife, that: "Actually, work never killed anybody. It's worry, booze, cigarettes and fat bellies that get 'em."

One of the nearly unnoticed vices which undercuts the work ethic is gambling. In Canada, at both provincial and federal government levels, it is proliferating at an alarming rate. And as University of Colorado Professor, Thomas Martinez, is pointing out, "America has been hit by a gambling 'epidemic' and it's spreading like wildfire. There's so much emphasis on gambling today that you can't get away from it. Since the end of World War II, both illegal and legal gambling have increased tremendously. In just the last 10 years, 15 states have set up lotteries. In the early 1960's, with the exception of Nevada, state-sanctioned gambling was practically limited to horse race betting. Today 44 states are involved in some form of legalized gambling—from casinos to cards to bingo to *jai alai* to lotteries. And the situation promises to get worse. Over half of the adult population now engages in some form of gambling, and the number of compulsive gamblers is between six and nine million. Martinez asserts that the states are to blame for much of this increase in betting activity because they're continuing to legalize gambling, viewing it "as a source of revenue acceptable to the tax-burdened public. And it isn't only the states, but the mass media," Martinez added. "Take television. There are some 45 hours of game shows a week on TV, and this contributes to gambling fever." Martinez fears the rise in gambling is going to create even more compulsive gamblers in the U.S.—wrecking uncounted lives. "People trip out on gambling. They fantasize about being big winners. They see themselves going off on great vacations, building hospitals in their name. They spend money they shouldn't. Some of them forge checks or even steal."

Msgr. Joseph A. Dunne, president of the National Council on Compulsive Gambling, says that America is being swept by a gambling epidemic and that people are being seriously harmed by it. "Off-track betting has been legalized in New York for four years, and in that time we've more than doubled the number of Gamblers Anonymous meetings. There's a real problem here," says Dunne.

Which brings us to the dire need for Christians to see to it that their faith in Christ affects the totality of their life-style. In 1978, an international conference of 800 delegates was assembled in California to discuss the matter of linking Christ's "Creation to Christian Creativity." In his keynote address, former President Gerald Ford lamented that, in spite of the fact that one-third of all North Americans claim to be born again, "three out of four of these people say they do not connect religion and their decisions about right and wrong." One of the exemplary applications of Christian faith to practice was articulated by the Ontario legislator Margaret Birch: "My personal faith is the core or my career as a politician. Given the pressures and responsibilities of being a Cabinet member, I couldn't get through each day without God's grace and power. Every day I face real moral decisions which make me fall back on my faith."

Dr. William Standish Reed of Tampa, Florida, is an example of someone who wants to see Christ paramount in the medical profession. He is Founder-President of the Christian Medical Foundation, whose aim is to put Christ at the controls of their medical practices. Their "aim is to provide the best in modern medicine, combined with a full Christian approach to people's spiritual and emotional needs."

Then there is the matter of giving. Jesus said: "Give, and it shall be given unto you; good measure, pressed down, and shaken together, and running over, shall men give into your bosom. For with the same measure that ye mete withal it shall be measured to you again" (Luke 6:38). That's a divine principle and a human privilege. Last year the average North American Christian gave $150 to the work of Christ. That's one-fifth of a tithe. Christ has greatly blessed His people with peace and prosperity on this continent. If we multiplied our giving by 5, and brought it up to full measure, would the Lord not bless us fivefold? I believe He would. D. L. Moody once said, "God will allow millions to pass through my hands for the work of God if none of it sticks to my hands." When the late R. G. LeTourneau was asked how it was that God had blessed his business so much as a maker of huge earth moving equipment, he replied that he had a shovel. And God had a shovel. And they were shovelling to each other. But God had a bigger shovel! I remember Richard Christy, in Belfast, in the fifties. He pastored a large church, and also ran a large and flourishing business. I asked him how he could cope. He replied that when he first began to work for Christ, he made a covenant with Him which went like this: "Lord, I'll look after your business, and You look after mine!"

9

Superior Judge

In *Superman*, one of the most remarkable scenes in the entire movie is when Superman seems to reverse his usual savior role. There is a speedboat full of criminals trying desperately to make their escape from the law by racing down the East River in New York, heading for open water and the ocean. They have seemingly eluded the long arm of the law. New York City's army of 10,000 policemen have lost them. But they have not eluded Superman! He overtakes them, picks up their whole boat and carries them, humiliated, through the air to Wall Street, where he sets them down, dripping wet, in the midst of the arresting officers, to be arraigned for judgment.

If there's one thing clear in the Bible, it is the fact that everyone on earth—of all generations and nations—will meet again on the occasion of the Judgment Day. Of course, the day of judgment will not be restricted to a 24-hour day as we know it. St. Peter writes in his last chapter that all are locked into a date with God: "Kept in store, reserved unto . . . the day of judgment": "be not ignorant of this one thing, that one day is with the Lord as a thousand years, and a thousand years, as one day" (2 Pet. 3:7, 8).

The Bible has nearly 400 references to the judgments of God and over 200 verses deal with God as Judge or use the word "judged." In Acts 17:31, St. Paul told the elitist Athenians that they should surely repent and turn to Christ, for God has "appointed a day in which he will judge the world in righteousness by that Man [Jesus] whom he hath ordained: Whereof he hath given assurance unto all men, in that he hath raised him from the dead" (Acts 17:31). Jesus spoke many times of the "day of judgment." He insisted that the people of Sodom and Gomorrha would be present "in the day of judgment" (Matt. 10:15), as would every population to which disciples went (see verses 14, 15). St. John wrote in the sunset years of his life that a man should live his life in such a way as to be able to "have boldness in the day of judgment" (1 John 4:17).

Ours is not an age in which the day of judgment gets a lot of attention in the media, in our political, economic, social or educational focuses, or indeed in our churches. The Apostles' Creed is quoted worldwide, in unison, in most Christian churches, every Sunday, clearly alluding to the fact that Christ "shall come to judge the quick and the dead." But the majority of sermons in both Catholic and Protestant churches today are all too often strangely silent on this theme. For example, it would be quite unusual to go into an Anglican church anywhere in the world today and hear the Vicar open with one hand to the Bible, and with his other, to the Common Book of Prayer and expound on your "hour of death, and in the day of judgment."

A hundred years ago classical literary scholars had no hesitation on this theme. A Charles Dickens would write: "I expect a judgement." An Emily Dickenson, writing on death, warned, "Make this bed with awe: in it wait till judgement break." Bayard Taylor in his

"Bedouin Song" alluded to: "Till the sun grows cold. And the stars are old. And the leaves of the judgement book unfold." Of course, Shakespeare constantly invoked the Judgement Day as the great leveler of man's earthly deeds. In *Hamlet* he refers to one who engages in immorality and murder, and one who "waits upon the judgement." In *Julius Caesar,* he assures that "men have lost their reason" when they allow: "O judgement! Thou are fled to brutish beasts." He asks warningly in *Measure for Measure*: "How would you be, if He which is the top of judgment should but judge you as you are?"

Many of the foremost observers of our contemporary scene are thinking about life being seasoned by the awareness of the Judgment Day. Winston Churchill grieved at the moral skid of post World War II Britain, as did the senior member of the House of Lords, Viscount Samuel. Both exhorted the clergy to resurrect the doctrine of a final judgment and thunder it from the pulpits throughout the land if Old Britannia would rise again. We in North America do well to remember that our legal oath derives from the old Scottish oath: "I pledge before Almighty God, before Whom I shall give answer in that Great Day of Judgement to tell the truth, the whole truth, and nothing but the truth: so help me God!" In Britain some judges have actually been insisting that in serious—e.g. murder trials—the whole of the old oath be reactivated.

Werner Von Braun's conversion took place because he came to believe that as there was a Nuremberg for the Nazis, so there would be a judgment day for everyone. Late in life he wrote of his new purpose in living: inspired by a "belief in a last judgement, when everyone of us has to account for what we did with God's great gift of life on the earth." He urged that we therefore "cherish the award or suffer the penalty decreed in a final judgement." Before his death, the late Pope Paul, addressing 100,000 people in St. Peter's Square, said that in his feeling "the fragility of human life," his mind was constantly occupied with "the fear of God's judgement at the moment of death," which "is always present and full of mystery."

"Is there a Judgement Day?" a front-page headline in *The Toronto Star*, for January 28, 1978, asks. The article is on "near death experiences [which] show that 'there may well be a final judgement,' says Raymond Moody in . . . the concluding excerpt from his book *Reflections on Life After Life*." Moody's earlier book, of course, *Life After Life*, had largely dealt with those who had been pronounced clinically dead, only to be revived and come back to tell of felicitous experiences in the beyond. *Reflections* (1978) undertakes to be more objective and present glimpses of those who came back having had horror as well as happy confrontations with impending judgment. Assesses Moody: "There may well be a final judgment; near-death experiences in no way imply the contrary. . . . I have never interviewed anyone who has been a real 'rounder' prior to his close call." Moody quotes one man who, insofar as his medical history is concerned, had "died" and then came back: "I was first out of my body, and I could see my body lying there. . . . Then it seemed that everything in my life went by for review, you might say. I was really very, very ashamed of a lot of the things. . . . It was as though a judgement was being made. . . . It was like I would experience an event with omnipotent knowledge helping me to see. It showed me not only what I had done, but how I had affected others. It wasn't like looking at a movie because I could feel these things;

not even your thoughts are lost . . . Every thought was there."

Moody quotes a woman who was medically "believed dead for 15 minutes." She reported that the people she saw—in the world beyond—"looked dull, gray. And they seemed to be forever shuffling and moving around, not knowing where they were going, not knowing who to follow, or what to look for. As I went by they didn't even raise their heads to see what was happening. They seemed to be thinking, 'Well, it's all over with. What am I doing?' 'What's it all about?' Just this absolute, crushed, hopeless deameanor—not knowing what to do or where to go or who they were or anything else."

Probably the bluntest book on this theme is *Beyond Death's Door* (1978) by Dr. M. S. Rawlings, whom *The Toronto Star* calls "one of the leading cardiologists in the United States." Rawlings describes how he "once believed 'religion was hocus-pocus.' But now that about one half of all sudden heart-related deaths can be restored to life through medical procedures, he has found that about 20 percent say they have had an experience of a life beyond. 'Previously, all we have heard about are the good experiences of such cases.' But Rawlings has found there are more bad experiences—experiences of hell—than good ones." This is certainly verified by Jesus' words, "Wide is the gate, and broad is the way, that leadeth to destruction, and many there be which go in thereat: because strait is the gate, and narrow is the way, which leadeth unto life, and few there be that find it" (Matt. 7:13, 14). A glance around our world via the media—or simply with open eyes—would confirm what our Lord said. *Damnation Alley,* as the current, widely publicized movie is entitled, is much more rushed than the strait and narrow way that leads to life.

The answer to the Judgment Day, Scripture says, is to turn to Christ now.

Doubtless the fullest passage in Scripture on this theme is Revelation 20:11-13 where we read that the aging John "saw a great white throne, and him that sat on it, from whose face the earth and the heaven fled away; and there was found no place for them. And I saw the dead, small and great, stand before God; and the books were opened; and another book was opened, which is the book of life: and the dead were judged out of those things which were written in the books, according to their works. And the sea gave up the dead which were in it; and death and hell delivered up the dead which were in them: and they were judged every man according to their works."

In a national magazine, I saw a picture of the place where Howard Hughes is buried. His plot was "completely unmarked" by design so as to remain anonymous. In the Judgment Day, God Almighty will not have difficulty finding the grave and body of Howard Hughes, or of anyone else who has ever inhabited this planet.

I cannot help but feel that God—who controls the flow of history as well as the lives of believers—permitted Watergate to happen to warn man that "it is appointed unto men once to die, but after this the judgment" (Heb. 9:27). *The New York Times* in retrospect has been recounting in 1978 how "Richard Nixon decided his presidency was doomed from the day the public learned his tape recorders eavesdropped on every conversation in his office. 'I believe,' writes Nixon in retrospect, 'that from the time of the disclosure of the existence of the tapes and my decision not to destroy them, my presidency had little chance of surviving to the end of its term.' " *The New York Times* went on to state that "once existence of the tapes became public knowledge, Nixon fought desperately to keep their content secret—a battle he finally lost in the U.S. Supreme Court. Before the Watergate scandal revelations, only a handful of Nixon's top aides knew he had installed microphones in his desk and in wall sconces in the Oval Office, in the cabinet room of the White House, in his hideaway office in the Executive Office Building and at Camp David, Md. A federal grand jury named Nixon an unindicted co-conspirator in the Watergate coverup and the Supreme Court ruled he had to give up the tapes for use in the coverup trial. Among the tapes were three conversations Nixon had with chief of staff H. R. Haldeman June 23, 1972—six days after the break-in at the Democratic Party headquarters. That day Nixon told Haldeman the CIA should tell the FBI to stay out of the Watergate investigation. That was the so-called 'smoking gun' conversation. Nixon, whose impeachment was scheduled for consideration by the House of Representatives, made the tape public Aug. 5, 1974. The reaction around the country and in Congress was so strong Nixon announced his resignation three days later."

In his well-known TV interviews with David Frost, Mr. Nixon disclosed how he felt when the worst of the Watergate disclosures were dredged up. He replied that he wished he wouldn't wake up in the morning.

Man will run for his entrenched intellectual "shelters" when the matter of judgment day is brought up. Yet he'll read with profound admiration and credibility H. G. Wells' *The Time Machine* which predicates an owner of a "Time Machine" who can thereby travel into the past or the future at will. The Time traveler's description of the people of the future, the weak Eloi and the predatory Morlocks, has its roots in some interesting scientific hypotheses. If a reader can fantasize on Wells, he or she ought to reflect with profound solemnity on the matter of the Judgment Day.

I was deeply moved by an interview I conducted with Barry McGuire in 1977: specially as it pertained to how indelibly he had God's Judgment Day written into his conscience, even at a time when he seemed farthest from God. Barry's "Eve of Destruction"—a kind of a sick commentary on earth's doomsday—was the top pop song in the world in the late sixties.

Barry was brought up in Oklahoma, hit Hollywood at the time Elvis Presley was on the rise, and in the mid to late sixties walked into the drugs and flower power culture. Looking at first from the bottom up, getting to the top certainly had its kicks. But atop the heap, he suddenly felt like he was on a roller coaster, that was—yes—lifting him, flipping him, twirling him, jiggling him and spinning him! But he soon found himself dizzy, flat and suicidal. A dozen of his buddies had taken their lives, because as they'd smoke grass, get loaded up on booze and immoralize, they'd always "just miss" having fun! They'd look into each other's eyes and see nothing behind them but bottomless pits.

Then one day a Jesus person met Barry and his friends on the street and said: "Hey you guys, remember Jesus!" And Barry couldn't get the statement out of his head for eight months. He stumbled on to a *Good News for Modern Man* Bible, and he couldn't seem to escape the compulsion to read it. Finally, one night in a friend's house in Laurel Canyon in Hollywood, he surrendered his all to Jesus Christ. Two or three days later he spent $7.50 of his last $12 on a ticket to his Christian uncle's house and, as Barry puts it, "Jesus rode out of town with me on that Greyhound Bus that afternoon." And Barry's been going with Him ever since. He was delivered from the force of sin by the force of faith in Christ, and by the fact that the same Jesus who one day will demand "that every knee should bow . . . and every tongue should confess that Jesus Christ is Lord, to the glory of God the Father" (Phil. 2:10, 11). That was the Christ who had regenerated Barry McGuire.

Jesus Christ himself will be the judge at Judgment Day. Jesus assured us that His Father had sent Him, not only to be the Savior of those who believe, but to be the final Judge of those who don't. He said, "For judgment I am come into this world" (John 9:39).

Jesus had a great deal to say about what and how He would judge, as well as where and when. He underlined: "Thou shalt not kill," insisting "whosoever shall kill shall be in danger of judgment." Furthermore, "Whosoever is angry with his brother without a cause shall be in danger of the judgment" (Matt. 5:21, 22). He taught: "Judge not, that ye be not judged. For with what judgment ye judge, ye shall be judged" (Matt. 7:1, 2). He warned: "Woe unto you, scribes and Pharisees, hypocrites! For ye pay tithe" but "have omitted the weightier matter" of "judgment" (Matt. 23:23). Jesus made it clear that in principle He was committed to "judge not according to the appearance, but judge righteous judgment" (John 7:24). Yes, when "I judge, my judgment is true" (John 7:16).

It seems to me that the most ancient quotation in all literature is the one in Jude 14, 15 where we read that "Enoch also, the seventh from Adam, prophesied of these saying, Behold, the Lord cometh with ten thousands of his saints, to execute judgment upon all, and to convince all that are ungodly among them of all their ungodly deeds which they have ungodly committed, and of all their hard speeches which ungodly sinners have spoken against him." The Old Testament writers were constantly alluding to the judgment of God. Hundreds of passages deal with this solemn theme.

Billy Graham often quotes his wife, Ruth, saying that if God Almighty does not bring the people of our generation to judgment, He would have to apologize to Sodom and Gomorrha.

The writer to the Hebrews taught that "eternal judgment" was a "doctrine" at the very "foundation" of our faith (Heb. 6:1, 2). He not only insisted that after death comes the judgment (Heb. 9:27) but that ungodly people who "sin willfully" after having "received the knowledge of the truth" spend their lives in "certain fearful looking for of judgment and fiery indignation" (Heb. 10:26, 27).

Of course, if the judgment involves no sentencing, it would not be a judgment to be feared. But Jesus assures us that it will be the ultimate assize of the universe, and it will be assembled for the joint purposes of vindicating God's righteousness and for sentencing impenitent sinners. In Matthew 25 we read of His solemn Word: that "when the Son of Man shall come in his glory, and all the holy angels with him, then shall he sit upon the throne of his glory: and before him shall be gathered all nations: and he shall separate them one from another, as a shepherd divideth his sheep from the goats: and he shall set the sheep on his right hand, but the goats on the left" (vv. 31-33).

That will be the great Y in the road to eternity. Look at those on Christ's left hand. "Then shall he say also unto them on the left hand, Depart from me, ye cursed, into everlasting fire prepared for the devil and his angels." And "these shall go away into everlasting punishment." Nor is this Jesus' only allusion to the "everlasting punishment" of the impenitent. Someone has listed the references Jesus made to heaven, and His references to hell, and concluded that our Lord spoke thirteen times as much about hell as about heaven.

Jesus often spoke of damnation. In His Great Commission He instructed that an integral part of our message was: "He that believeth not shall be damned" (Mark 16:16). Referring to the Judgment Day, Jesus warned that "they that have done evil . . . shall come forth . . . unto the resurrection of damnation" (John 5:29). He explained that such a damnation is everlasting: "He that shall blaspheme against the Holy Ghost hath never forgiveness, but is in danger of eternal damnation" (Mark 3:29). Especially on religious hypocrites did Jesus pronounce anathema: "Woe unto you, scribes and Pharisees, hypocrites! for ye devour widows houses, and for a pretense make long prayer: Therefore ye shall receive the greater damnation" (Matt. 23:14). In even more scathing denunciation our Lord asked: "Ye serpents, ye generation of vipers, how can ye escape the damnation of hell?" (Matt. 23:33).

Some theologians have implied that St. Paul backed off considerably from Jesus' strong statements on eternal punishment. That is not true. St. Paul wrote to Timothy of young women who "wax wanton against Christ" and so, destine themselves to "damnation" (1 Tim. 5:11, 12). To the Corinthians he wrote that he who takes the communion bread and wine without getting right with God "eateth and drinketh damnation to himself" (1 Cor. 11:29). To the Romans he wrote that those who treat the laws of the land criminally "shall receive to themselves damnation" (Rom. 13:2); and that those who say: "Let us do evil, that good may come" their "damnation is just" (Rom.

3:8). Speaking of the last days, previous to the return of Christ to defeat the Antichrist, Paul wrote to the Thessalonians of those who would live in "all deceivableness of unrighteousness in them that perish; because they received not the love of the truth, that they might be saved. And for this cause God shall send them strong delusion, that they should believe a lie: that they all might be damned who believed not the truth, but had pleasure in unrighteousness" (2 Thess. 2:10-12).

To close themselves off from thinking about perdition, people treat it as a whimsical place, more of a joke than an eschatological reality. It is fashionable to treat the whole theme as a fictional domain, created from one part Dante and one part Milton with a dash of religious art thrown in. The *U.S. Catholic* states that "hell has become so trivialized that it has even lost its force as a curse. 'Go to hell' is a suggestion friends share. 'The hell it is' is an exclamation of surprise and incredulity. 'Dammit' is something we utter when we stub our toes, not an eternal sentence!" The conclusion arrived at is that "a people who care about God will not have to worry about hell." True! insofar as the true Christian is concerned. But untrue if the people of God who are Christ's care about the people who are not Christ's. After all, it was Christ who said: "He that believeth not shall be damned!" (Mark 16:16).

A generation ago, sophisticated Christians largely abandoned the fire aspects of hell. Now many are wondering. Jesus said that for those who "shall be cast out into outer darkness: there shall be weeping and gnashing of teeth" (Matt. 8:12). On another occasion, He said—actually three times over—that for those "cast into hell fire: where their worm dieth not, and the fire is not quenched" (Mark 9:43-48). Now how could that be? asked thinkers when I was a boy. Their only knowledge of fire was that of oxidation. How could there be fire and darkness at the same time? And how could people burn and not be consumed? All one can do is to take very seriously such inventions as, say, the microwave oven. Twelve percent of North American homes now have microwave ovens which can cook a meal in a fraction of the time it takes an ordinary oven to do so. Furthermore, a microwave oven cooks from the inside out, rather than vice-versa; and in a microwave oven when the heat is intense and totally penetrating, the oven itself is as black as a stygian night. This is not to say that hell is a microwave oven, but it does cancel out some of the old so-called scientific objections to hell-fire.

In 1978, President Carter has made a great deal out of the Neutron Bomb. It's supposed to destroy people while preserving things. What if fire is discovered by technology which preserves people, while otherwise acting as fire? Let us not be unaware of what science, in the short span of one generation, has turned up about nuclear fire, and laser beams. Who knows? I don't. God does. And He warns us to stay out of hell. Meanwhile, let's not tamper with doctrines which Jesus Christ so clearly set forth.

Perhaps the greatest contribution to church growth in the world in our generation has been made by Dr. James Kennedy, minister of the huge Coral Ridge Presbyterian Church in Fort Lauderdale, Florida, and author of *Evangelism Explosion.*

Dr. Kennedy and I were having breakfast in Memphis together in May, 1978. He told me of Jim, a businessman in his early 60's, who had lived for 50 years as an agnostic. Then one day, he was rushed to the North Ridge Cardiac Hospital, in Fort Lauderdale, with a severe heart attack. He died—clinically, for several minutes—and then was resuscitated by the artificial respiration technique currently being advocated by the American Heart Association.

Alive (again, if you will) he sought and had an interview with Dr. Kennedy. He claimed he had been in the region of hell. There was darkness, yet fire everywhere. The pain was unbearable. "How severe was the pain?" asked Dr. Kennedy. Jim told him that it was a thousand times worse than he had ever experienced on earth. Asked about what pain he had ever felt on earth, he pulled up both pant legs. One was a wooden leg. The other was covered with burnt scar tissue. Jim said that this had happened some years before when a gallon of gasoline was on a shelf in his garage. Accidentally, as he went to back his car out, he had bumped it off the shelf. It spilled all over him and then ignited into fire. But the fires of hell, Jim insisted, were a thousand times worse than the third-degree burns he had sustained from the garage disaster.

There is a current film advertising "The Last Waltz." Any moment now could be your last waltz. There was that terribly tragic fire they had in the Supper Club in Covington, Kentucky, where John Davidson and 1300 night-clubbers were jammed in. After the fire had broken out, a fire boy lept to the stage and cried, "Fire! Fire! Get Out!" Most just laughed, dismissing it as just another gag. But 362 perished in the flames. Jesus said, "But I will forewarn you whom to fear; fear him who after he hath killed, hath power to cast into hell. I say unto you fear him."

There's been a film showing around the Continent recently entitled *Mansion of the Doomed.* The Bible doesn't tell us that hell is a mansion. It's a furnace. Another movie is *The Sentinel,* and it has a cross in the middle with the byline: "There Must Forever Be a Guardian at the Gate of Hell: The Sentinel."

Christians are sentinels warning people to stay out of hell. There's a book title *Drop Into Hell.* Christians are to urge people *not* to drop into hell.

I saw a bumper sticker the other day which asked: "What do you miss by being Christian? Hell!" And I thought: That's a bit blunt. But it's what Jesus taught. I'm no expert on hell, but I know what the Bible says: "Fear hath torment" (1 John 4:18). "Sinners," wrote the ancient Isaiah (33:14), "are afraid; fearfulness hath surprised the hypocrites. Who among us shall dwell with the devouring fire? Who among us shall dwell with everlasting burnings?"

Which leads me to say that I'm glad Jesus didn't just say He'd be consigning Christ rejectors to hell. He said that at the judgment, He'd "say unto them on his right hand, Come, ye blessed of my Father, inherit the kingdom prepared for you from the foundation of the world" (Matt. 25:34). Johnny Carson ended one of his "Tonight" tapings with the wish: "Have a Happy Eternity." Actually it's only Jesus who is qualified to confer a "happy eternity" on people.

Comedian Woody Allen was asked by an interviewer: "Aren't you happy that you will achieve immortality through your achievements?" To which Woody gloomily replied, "Who cares about achieving immortality through achievements? I'm interested in achieving immortality through not dying." That's only possible, Woody, if you're a Christian.

What people are craving for today according to *The Chicago Sun Times* columnist "Dear Miss Graham" is a know-so about eternal life. She writes: "I'm still struggling. I don't *know* with absolute certainty about life everlasting. I wish I did." St. Paul wrote: "We *know* that if our earthly house of this tabernacle were dissolved, we have a building of God, a house not made with hands, eternal in the heavens"

(2 Cor. 5:1). Even the eminent Swiss psychiatrist, and the world's foremost expert on death, Dr. Kubler Ross, said recently, "I used to say: 'I believe in life after death.' Now I know."

We're reading, as we've noted, a lot about Raymond Moody's *Life After Life*. I actually prefer D. L. Moody's testimony. As he lay dying, the week before the nineteenth century gave way to the twentieth, he exulted: "They'll publish it in the newspapers: Moody Dead. But Moody won't be dead. He'll just have begun to live. Earth is receding. Heaven approaching. God is calling me!"

Baden-Powell's widow, who died at 88 recently, was the wife of the founder of the Boy Scouts, a movement which sprang second generation out of Moody's evangelism. Mrs. Baden-Powell had said: "As long as I can still be of use, that's all that matters in life. Then I'll be united with [my husband] again." It reminded me of the account of Phil Jenks dying words: "Easy dying! Blessed dying! Glorious dying! I have experienced more happiness in two hours today dying than in my whole life." John Lyth on his deathbed exclaimed: "Can this be death? Why, it is better than living! Tell them I die happy in Jesus." Dr. Cullen exulted as he approached the Pearly Gates: "I wish I had the power of writing. I would describe how pleasant it is to die."

In 1964, I held a Billy Graham Associate Crusade in Northern Maine. Several hundred came forward to give their lives to Christ. The organist's father was still in his 40's. He had not been a church-goer. On the very last night of the crusade he attended and amidst a great spiritual harvest he came forward with the many others to settle his accounts with Christ. Hardly two weeks later I received a letter from his daughter. Her father had dropped dead on the sidewalk on the Thursday following the crusade. But, she rejoiced, "he's with Jesus!"

During the autumn of 1978, Pope John Paul I, after only 34 days in office was found dead in bed. In his last public utterance, he was discussing Christianity and communism. His final statement was: "The chief teaching of Jesus Christ was eternal life!"

10

Super Savior

So where does man begin being reconciled to God through Christ? He begins by confessing that he is a sinner.

General Charles DeGaulle, who tried so hard to restore the grandeur of France, lamented before his death that Frenchmen have in them the seeds of their own destruction. That's true of all people. Eric Hoffer, in his widely quoted *Newsweek* interview, confessed that at heart "I am a savage." We all are! And well meaning though we may be, as *The Cedar Valley Times* in Iowa editorializes: "politicians who promise to clean things up are usually on a soap box." Soup, soap and socialism can never cleanse people who are conquered from within by sin. Instinctively, people search for God with something of the enthusiasm of a thief looking for a policeman. People are people, and as St. Paul put it, on their own essentially "all seek their own, not the things which are Jesus Christ's" (Phil. 2:21). And again, "There is none righteous, no not one; there is none that understandeth, there is none that seeketh after God. They are all gone out of the way, they are together become unprofitable; there is none that doeth good, no, not one" (Rom. 3:10-12). So where does this leave man? Jesus warned: "Except ye repent, ye shall all likewise perish" (Luke 13:3). Hua Kwa Feng, China's head, remonstrates that the trouble with the Chinese is so many "have refused to repent." If that's true of hard-line communism, how much more true it is of Christianity. "Sorry seems to be the hardest word," sings Elton John. Eric Segal, the Yale professor who became famous as the author of *Love Story*, defines love as never having to say you're sorry. Coming to Christ, as Billy Graham has demonstrated in his prayer with millions of repenting sinners, must begin with: "I am sorry for my sins," or words to that effect.

We received a letter from the Detroit area, which tells us of someone recently giving their life to Christ. It reads: "Since that time my life has *changed*. It has *changed* just as you said it would when I accepted Christ. My new attitude toward other people, the contentment I have inside, the joy and happiness, are just a few of the new emotions I am experiencing. I am sorry I didn't make my commitment sooner, because I feel I have wasted so much time. No one understands what is happening to me, no one except those who have been through the experience themselves. People cling to their belief that they want to worship and accept God on their own terms—the way they see fit. That is the belief I used to carry. I didn't want to be a hypocrite, so I wouldn't give myself to God fully. I gave only as much as I wanted. But I found out that you can't have an experience with God on your terms; it has to be on his terms. And it was so simple, as you said, to cross over that line from death to life."

So man is a sinner. And because he is a sinner, he is separated from God. Isaiah, the ancient prophet, put his finger on it when he wrote: "Your iniquities have separated between you and your God, and your sins have hid his face from you that he will not hear"

(Isa. 59:1, 2). You see, the writer to the Hebrews assured that Jesus Christ is "holy, harmless, undefiled, separate from sinners" (Heb. 7:26) and that "without holiness no man shall see the Lord" (Heb. 12:14). So man has to make a choice. He has to separate from his sins or remain separated from his God. St. Paul put it plainly to the Corinthians: "Wherefore come out from among them, and be ye separate, saith the Lord, and touch not the unclean thing; and I will receive you and will be a Father to you, and ye shall be my sons and daughters, saith the Lord Almighty" (2 Cor. 6:17, 18).

Often a person begins to be haunted about the matter of death and eternal life. Glen Campbell, on Johnny Carson's program one night, blurted out: "What do you do to get eternal life?" Patrick Henry, the comedian, was on with Johnny a few nights later and he remarked with astonishing candor that everyone wants to go to heaven (but) everyone wants booze, illicit sex and gambling, and you can't have it both ways, I guess." The Bible doesn't say: "I guess." It affirms: "I know!"

We received a letter from a woman in Saskatchewan, a wife, who was ready to walk out of her marriage. Her life, she says, was "dark, confused, nervous, bitter, angry." She was on pills for various emotional ills. Then she received the Gospel. She wrote in for counseling, and we wrote to her, addressing her specific needs. Then, after reading that reply she wrote: "I . . . found Christ as my Saviour and Lord. What a *change* has taken place in my life. Now I am happy and relieved. . . . I call on the Lord and He is right there to help me. It's almost too good to be true!"

All have sinned. All are separated thereby from God. None seeks God instinctively. But God calls to all by His Holy Spirit. He calls us by His challenge to change us in His Word. He calls us to make a choice. He calls to us by telling us that we must get rid of our sins, or they will get rid of us. But we cannot cleanse ourselves from our sins, from the guilt which gnaws at every Christless soul.

Joan Crawford is dead, and Charles Castle has written her popular biography. In it he tells how she was born illegitimate, and left home early because of the sexual harassments from her mother's boyfriend. Her name was "LeSeuer." It sounded too much like "sewer," so she changed it. When she made it in Hollywood, Castle recounts that "like Harriet Craig, she became a paranoid about cleanliness and hygiene," which her psychiatrists put down to "an attempt to wash away guilt or atone for forbidden desires." She carried her own sheets to the finest hotels and "scrubbed and disinfected everything, often down on her knees herself to re-do a floor already scrubbed by her staff." Like Shakespeare's MacBeth shrieking: "Out, damned spot!" Joan Crawford was trying to get rid of her sins. But from Pilate to Crawford, washing with water never cleanses from sin. Psychiatrists are now saying that the 2.8 billion dollars North Americans currently spend on detergents and bath soap has many spiritual implications: often it's an effort to get rid of sin.

In 1978 we read for the first time from the 1947 diary of William Lyon MacKenzie King (the longest serving of Canadian Prime Ministers). The day that his fondly endeared dog died, he wrote that its death for him was like the "crucifixion of Christ all over. I felt as if he had died for me, that my sins might be forgiven me." What would make the man, whom some think of as our greatest Canadian ever, write a thing like that? The guilt of sin! The same guilt which caused two Filipinos to have themselves nailed to crosses last Easter. Or the same guilt which is causing North Americans to run chronically to physicians incurring doctors' bills which are rising twice as fast as the overall cost of living. The medical profession itself assures us constantly that 70% of their patients have nothing organically wrong with them beyond spiritual guilt.

So man does need Christ—the Jesus Christ who as God the Son spanned the gulf between man and his Maker. Recently a Jewish rabbinical leader said, "In Judaism we believe in the necessity of the mercy of God, but a Jewish believer cannot predict how or when God will be merciful. Christianity, on the other hand, locates the mercy of God in Jesus Christ." This is precisely Paul's teaching, who wrote to the Galatians that "when the fulness of the time was come, God sent forth his Son, made of a woman, made under the law, to redeem them that were under the law, that we might receive the adoption of sons. And because ye are sons, God hath sent forth the Spirit of his Son into your hearts, crying Abba, Father. Wherefore thou art no more a servant, but a son, and if a son, then an heir of God through Christ" (Gal. 4:4-7).

We have already quoted from Ephesians. To the Philippians Paul wrote: "Christ Jesus . . . being in the form of God, thought it not robbery to be equal with God: but made himself of no reputation, and took upon him the form of a servant, and was made in the likeness of men: and being found in fashion as a man, he humbled himself, and became obedient unto death, even the death of the cross. Wherefore God also hath highly exalted him and given him a name which is above every name: that at the name of Jesus every knee should bow of things in heaven, and things in earth, and things under the earth; and that every tongue should confess that Jesus Christ is Lord to the glory of God the Father" (Phil. 2:5-11).

In the film, Superman welds the Golden Gate Bridge back together. Jesus on the cross, as the Son of God, repaired the broken bridge between God and man. Early in this century in Scotland, there was a drawbridge over a river, over which a people-packed passenger train passed. A boat came down the river. The drawbridge operator raised the bridge, all the while holding to the lever without which the drawbridge would not move. The boat barely through, the packed train came around the bend, ahead of schedule, blew its whistle, and the operator barely had time to get the bridge down if the lives of the train passengers were to be saved. But just at that point, his tiny son fell into the river, precisely as the train whistle blew. Unable to swim, the wee boy cried up: "Father, save me!" For the anguished father, it was his son or the trainload of people! He could not at the same time save his son and close the river bridge. And the train could not stop. His son gave his life, as a grieving father held onto his lever and got the bridge together, just as the onrushing train swept through.

The cross of Christ is where our Lord closed the bridge between God and man. But the cost was an awful one: "God so loved the world that he gave his only begotten Son" (John 3:16).

That center cross stands solitary and sentinel in a world, alienated from God, to call us to our Maker. It is the tower of power where man must initially meet his God. The 402-foot-high NASA Space Tower at Kennedy Space Center in Florida is now for sale. It was erected at a cost of 26.6 million dollars, scaffold-style, to launch man to the moon. The rocket which was spiked to it unleashed as much power as a string of bumper to bumper cars from Boston to Seattle. But it got rusty and had no further use. Jesus, spiked to the tower of Calvary's cross once and for all, launched man for heaven. That's the meaning of the old rugged cross. In Toronto, we have the world's tallest single standing structure, the 1814-foot CN Tower. You can eat up there in a revolving restaurant. But really, it's a communication tower for TV antennas, and soon is to be transmitting in 18 tongues—sort of trying to reverse the Tower of Babel. Jesus, from the tower of Calvary's cross communicates—in all languages: "Father, forgive them; they know not what they do!" And to those who receive His forgiveness and salvation, He assures: "Thou shalt be with me in paradise!" *The National Enquirer* claims that the public—on national television—would welcome the sight of public executions up on a tower of some kind. I wouldn't. Because by faith I saw the Man on the Center Cross, the Calvary Tower of Power, taking my place; and I've been forever changed.

When our sons were small boys in Oxford, England, they played three trumpets and sang. Once they were on Scottish television. When they finished, one of them asked a kindly, but eventually exasperated, engineer: "How can one person stand before one camera, and speak to one microphone, and the whole world see and hear him?" The man pointed to the Kirk O Shotts TV Tower and said: "It goes up and out from there. I can't explain it, but I know it works." I can't explain how the Tower Power from the Center Cross of Calvary can be transmitted to man across time and space: the forgiveness, cleansing, reconciliation to God and everlasting life, but I know it works.

When we were there in Scotland, one Sunday evening I was preaching in the Odeon Theatre in Glasgow. A distinguished Queen's Counsellor came forward to receive Christ. He had just received a special trophy for his legal expertise from Queen Elizabeth. But he had never yet been to the cross. Yes, he was a member of the Church of Scotland, but he himself said he had never really personally experienced Jesus Christ as his Savior and Lord. That night he encountered what Elisha Hoffman wrote about a century ago, and has since set millions to singing: "Have you been to Jesus for the cleansing power; are you washed in the blood of the Lamb?"

God can be known in Christ by all who come to Him. "Jesus Christ the Son of God," wrote St. Paul, is the "One to say 'Yes' " (1 Cor. 1:19) to those who come to Him. Desi Arnaz, Jr. stars in "The Voyage of Yes" on television. You can be on "The Voyage of Yes" with Christ if you will come to Him. *Come* is currently the title of a top best seller. The Bible tells us some 700 times to come to the Lord. When Homer James led David Mainse forward to give his life to Christ in the Glebe Street Auditorium in Ottawa 25 years ago, David recalls that the verse the counselor used was John 6:37: "Him that cometh unto me, I will in no wise cast out." Barry Mannilow is singing "It's daybreak, if you wanta believe." Spiritually this may be your daybreak—if you will believe on Christ.

Mao Tse Tung advanced the saying: "If we have a correct theory but merely prate about it, pigeonhole it, and do not put it into practice, then that theory, however good, is of no significance." To come to Christ you cannot merely theologize, philosophize, or fantasize on being a Christian. You have to firmly place your faith in Him, and do it now. It's a deliberate, decisive act of belief.

And to be Christ's means to be changed. Jesus Christ changes people—and through people the world: not the reverse.

Christ will change your life-style and your eternity

if you will give yourself fully to Him. President Carter's favorite song is John Newton's "Amazing Grace, how sweet the sound, that saved a wretch like me; I once was lost, but now am found; was blind but now I see."

I would like to ask you quite deliberately, Are you sure you have entrusted your life fully to Christ? If you are not sure, I'd like to point you to Him now.

In a crusade in Texas I mislaid my motel room key, and a man named Curtis Feelberg came to my aid with a master key. As we strolled over to open my locked door he said, "Dr. White, I'd like to lead you to your door and unlock it for you, because you led me to *the* Door, Jesus, and unlocked the way to heaven for me."

In the same way, I would like to lead you to the Door, Jesus. He said: "I AM the door."

To enter the Kingdom of Christ, the true Superman, there are certain steps to be taken:

The first step is to deliberately and wholeheartedly change your mind about your life of sin. The Bible calls this repentance. It is not shallow, like a New Year's resolution. It is a basic change of heart. It says, in effect, "God, there is not a single sin in my life which I want to repeat. There is not a solitary sinful practice which I want to hang onto."

The second step is to act upon that change of heart by confessing all your disobediences to God, one by one, as thoroughly as memory enables you to do. This is the beginning of a new, first-time, total honesty with God.

The third step is to receive Christ as Lord and Savior. You do this in prayer, simply telling God that He can take over every part of your life. When He comes in, Christ will give you inner assurance that your sins have been forgiven. Furthermore, He will let you know that eternal life is yours and that you are part of His great, world-wide spiritual family. The Bible is very clear about these steps, so you can count on God responding to you as you take them.

It really does not matter if you have considered yourself religious or irreligious up to this time in your life. It does not matter that you may have even thought of yourself as "Christian" in some vague sense. What *does* matter is that you take these steps *now*, and then attach yourself to a local church where these truths are taught and where you can get continuing help for your soul.

If you have taken these measures, I would like to invite you to write and tell me about it:

Dr. John Wesley White
Box 1000
Milliken, Ontario, Canada